PAPA'S
Stories

BRIAN MARCUS

ISBN 978-1-68197-919-9 (Paperback)
ISBN 978-1-68197-920-5 (Digital)

Copyright © 2016 by Brian Marcus

All rights reserved. No part of this publication may be reproduced, distributed, or transmitted in any form or by any means, including photocopying, recording, or other electronic or mechanical methods without the prior written permission of the publisher. For permission requests, solicit the publisher via the address below.

Christian Faith Publishing, Inc.
296 Chestnut Street
Meadville, PA 16335
www.christianfaithpublishing.com

Printed in the United States of America

Foreward

John and Colleen Musselman

The need and requirement that children be instructed in the things of God by parents, grandparents, and other Christian leaders is expressed in Deuteronomy 6, with these words: "You shall teach them diligently to your children, and shall talk of them when you sit in your house, and when you walk by the way, and when you lie down, and when you rise"—in other words, in every place and at every time.

Dr. J. I. Packer said of the great Puritan pastor Richard Baxter that he insisted that ministers must not only preach the Gospel but also "must do personal work, and deal with individuals one by one, because preaching alone often fails to bring things home to ordinary people." If Baxter is correct, as Packer insists he is, then "it will not be beyond us to find a method of doing it that suits our situation."

In writing *Papa's Stories*, Brian Marcus has found a practical, conversational, and engaging way to teach God's Word to his grandchildren so that each one of them would know God, believe the Gospel, and spend eternity with Christ. What reward could be better than for him to hear his granddaughter Anna say, "the Old Testament began to make sense to me," as her papa told the great redemptive stories of the Bible with imagination, passion, clarity, and loving engagement—along with some delicious chocolate ice cream!

If you could use some help in learning how to train up your child(ren) in the way he should go, I encourage you to get a copy of Brian Marcus's book *Papa's Stories: God's Promise of Salvation*, and set aside some time each evening to begin forming a Christian worldview in the mind and heart of your child.

-John Musselman

Preface

Brian and Donna Marcus

I am a most fortunate person. I have been happily married for over forty-five years. My wife and I have three beautiful and healthy daughters. They've all graduated from college and have married outstanding young men who love them. We now enjoy seven beautiful and healthy granddaughters.

    Every day, I find myself praying for the continued health and welfare of my family. I have seen many families decimated by tragedies. I know that everybody will face health issues or financial difficulties at some point. But the issues that I fear the most are spiritual. This world is infected with an evil spirit who is always trying hard to lead people into temptation. Adultery, pornography, dishonesty, anger, drug abuse, and all other sorts of sinful behavior can be more devastating to a family than any health or financial issue. Knowing that you are a child of God is the best protection against sinful behavior. I am dedicated, as a grandfather, to help all my children and grandchildren understand this correct world view.

I want to leave my children and grandchildren a legacy—something to remember me long after I'm gone. I want them to know what I've learned about life and what's important to me. That is my motivation in writing the following stories.

I believe that the Bible is the Word of God. It is absolute truth. The following stories are all based on the Bible. In order to make these stories interesting to my young granddaughters, I use a conversational method of writing. I try to simplify the big concepts that the Bible teaches and make them understandable to young children. To the best of my ability, my version of the stories do not conflict with the Truth that God teaches in the Bible. However, I am a fallible and sinful man, and if my stories teach any untruths, I am sincerely sorry.

It is my intent to personally read these stories to each of my granddaughters when they reach the age of twelve. My hope is that each of their hearts will be open to the Truth in the Word of God and they will be able to fend off the evil forces that this world will confront them with. With God's help, each of these precious children will spend eternity with Him—and with me.

Anna was only ten years old at the time that *Papa's Stories* was originally written. Lily was seven. Now, in 2016, Anna is fifteen and Lily twelve. Anna has joined Perimeter Church as a member, is an excellent home-schooled student, and is an amazing artist. Lily is one of the most popular kids at Perimeter School and one of the joys of my life.

Introduction by Anna

Lily and Anna Conroy

My name is Anna Conroy, and I am the granddaughter of Brian Marcus, who is known to me and my sister, Lily, as Papa. Papa is a good storyteller, and several years ago, when I was ten and Lily seven, Papa told us a series of well-known stories that were from the Old Testament. Starting with the Creation Story, Papa got us to really imagine what it must have been like for Adam and Eve to walk in Paradise and talk directly with God. He made us really think about what a terrible jolt it must have been when they were expelled from the garden and had to live with fear and danger, hard work and pain, death and disease. Could they remember what it had been like in the garden?

I never could understand the story of Cain and Abel. The Bible says that God accepted Abel's offering and rejected Cain's. The next thing you know, Cain kills his brother and God expels him from the land. But after hearing Papa tell the story, I really began to understand why God rejected Cain. I also began to see the big picture of the war that is taking place in the hearts of men, the war between good and evil. I began to see how Satan influences people, even me.

As Papa told the stories of Noah's Flood and then Abraham and Isaac and the beginning of the Nation of Israel, the Old Testament began to make sense to me. The Old Testament is not just a bunch of independent stories with some things to learn about life. The Old Testament is the story of the creation of man and of the fall of man and how man is born into a world that is separated from God and under the influence of God's enemy, Satan.

By the time Papa finished all the stories, I really understood who I was and who I wanted to be. I understood my own need of a Savior, and who that Savior is. I made a decision that will change my life forever. I have already begun to change.

Papa's Stories Study Guide

Each chapter ends with a short study guide. You will read together a familiar Old Testament story and the corresponding Papa's story. The important topics that these stories raise, provide an excellent opportunity for you to have really meaningful spiritual discussions with your child. Papa's Final Comment: This is the most important time you can possibly spend with your child!

Chapter 1

Beginnings

God Prepared a Special World for Man

Genesis 1 and 2, John 1:1–5
God Created All Things
Man Was Created Special
God Wants to Walk Closely with Man Forever

"Papa, Papa, can you tell us a story?" asked ten-year-old Anna when she saw that Papa had put down the book that he had been reading.

Papa was charged with watching Anna and her little sister, Lily, for a couple of hours while Grammy and their mother, Sally, went out on a shopping trip.

"I'd love to tell you a story, but the one I have in mind will take quite a while to tell, and you'll have to really use your imagination. Lily, turn off the TV and sit over here by Papa."

Lily turned off the TV and promptly jumped up on Papa's lap. "What's the story about, Papa?" she asked.

"You're going to go on a really long trip with me. This is not a trip to a place but a trip back in time. Way, way back in time. This story has a title. It's called 'The Beginning.' Do you two want to take this trip with me?"

"You're really weird, Papa," said Anna. "But Lily and I will take this so-called trip with you, won't we, Lily?"

"Sure, I like Papa's stories," Lily replied.

"You both have to close your eyes and think really hard," Papa began. "Think way, way back in time—to a time before there were any cars or planes or trains. There were no computers, or even TV. Can you imagine life before TV?" Papa laughed. "Now this is only the beginning of our trip back in time. We have to go a whole lot further back. Think of a time way before Columbus discovered America—even before Jesus walked in Jerusalem. Now think of when Moses came down the mountain with the Ten Commandments. Keep going back and back. Finally, we reach a time where there were only two people on the entire planet Earth—"

"I know! I know, Papa!" interrupted Lily. "We would be in the Garden of Eden. Isn't that where it all began?"

Papa smiled at his little granddaughter. "Very good, Lily. You've learned your Sunday school lessons very well. But that is not where I want us to stop on our trip back in time. I want to go back even further. Try to think of a time before there was no planet Earth, no moon, no sun, no stars. There was no morning or evening, no sky, nothing that you could see, touch, or smell—not even any time. Can you imagine it?"

Anna looked at her Papa with a funny face. "You really are weird, Papa. But yes, I can imagine it."

"I can too, Papa. But this story is starting to give me a headache," complained Lily.

"It's really hard to imagine 'no time' because we've lived our entire lives with time ticking away. Let's get back to the story. There isn't anything anywhere, but there is something. What do you think that something is?"

"God?" Anna asked.

"Excellent answer, Anna! Before He created the universe, God is the only thing that exists—and He can't be seen or touched or heard—but He does have the ability to do things. He knows everything, and He can make things come into existence simply by thinking. Before we go any further with this story, I have to tell you something. I know that all of this is true because the Bible says it is. The Bible is a book that God has given people so that we can learn things about Him. And in the Bible, God teaches us important stuff that we could never ever figure out by ourselves.

"The Bible says that God was there even before time began, or before the universe existed. God had a grand idea. His idea was to create a universe. Because God is all-powerful, all God has to do is think something into existence, and poof, there it is. His grand idea included stars, the moon, the earth, oceans, mountains, mornings, and evenings. He thought of time—hours and minutes, days and years.

God wanted living things in His Creation, and living things needed a place to live, or they would be lost in space. He created the planet Earth to be this special place. He made sure that it wasn't too hot or too cold. Plants and animals need food, sunshine, and water in order to live, so God had to make sure that everything that we would need would be there.

Then God made the stars, the sun, and the planets. By His will, He created a beautiful garden on planet Earth. The garden was filled with all kinds of trees, beautiful flowers, delicious apples, and juicy blueberries. When God does something, He does it perfectly and He doesn't forget anything.

When He made the animals and people they would need food and the plants would already be there. Next He filled the seas with all kinds of fish—big fish and small fish. He created birds and the sky was filled with beautiful flying creatures. He created animals of all kinds, from the great and powerful to the tiny and shy. Big bears, lions, giraffes, wolves, squirrels started to run through the beautiful gardens.

When God looked over all that He had created, He was very pleased with His work. He said to Himself, 'everything that I've made is excellent, and the world is now ready for the most important part of my creation—man.' He thought of people beginning with one man, He could see a future with black people, white people, Indians, Asians, and Hispanic. He saw happy times and sad times, fun days at the beach, scratched knees and broken arms, good report cards and smiling Moms, disobedient kids and angry Dads. He saw it all and He loved it. He even planned that you, Anna and you, Lily would be sitting here today listening to me tell this story. By His awesome power, He brought it all into existence!"

"Why was man the most important part of the creation Papa?" Anna asked.

That's a good question, Anna. The Bible teaches us that God's main reason for making the universe was to create man. Man would be special and different from all of the other creatures. The Bible says that man was created in the Image of God and that man would be given the assignment of taking care of God's creation. As God's managers, it is our job to take good care of the creation. He also asked us to find husbands and wives and have families. As His special children, God designed us to have a special relationship with Him. He would love us and care for us and at the same time we should obey Him and take care of the beautiful creation that He gave us to enjoy. God created man with a special soul that would have a personal relationship with God and both man's body and his soul were created to live forever."

"So Adam and Eve walked in the beautiful garden and enjoyed the excellent food that grew abundantly. They enjoyed their special relationship with God they loved Him and happily did what He asked of them and they loved each other."

"What would living in this garden be like, Papa?" asked Lily.

Papa scratched his head, and then finally answered, "We can only imagine what it was like but I have an idea that it was amazing. Imagine this scene: Adam and Eve are walking along through their beautiful garden. As Adam holds out his arm a beautiful hawk swoops down and lands lightly on his forearm, careful not to scratch Adam's skin with his talons. Eve picks a beautiful red berry from a nearby bush and the Hawk carefully accepts the gift and flies off to soar on the air currents high over the land. As they continue their walk they see a large field where a family of lions and a small herd of horses are grazing together. Two of the young lions chase and play with one of the young horses and after a few minutes of frantic playing, all three of them walk down to a small stream and get a drink from the fresh cool water."

"Why would the lions play with the horses Papa? Aren't lions and horses enemies?"

"That is a great question Anna. In the beginning, when God created His perfect paradise, the plants and grasses in the garden provided all the food that the animals ever needed. Even the hunger of the lions and tigers was perfectly satisfied. The only reason those animals are 'enemies' today is because the tigers and lions can't find the food that they need from the plants. Now they see other animals as food and they have to kill other animals in order to live. Something happened in the garden to change that world of perfect peace into a world where there is lots of fighting and stress. What happened didn't only affect the animals, but it affected people as well. We'll talk about that more in the next story."

Papa smiled at the two girls. "That is the end of my first story, 'The Beginning' I hope you enjoyed it."

Lily raised her hand, "I have a question Papa. If Adam and Eve were created to live forever, what happened to them?"

"That's a great question Lily. That question brings me to the next story. It's called 'Paradise Lost'. There are many more stories to tell. Let me know when you're ready for the next one."

Study Guide for Chapter 1- Beginnings

Story 1: The Beginning
Read: Genesis 1 and 2, and John 1:1-5
Read: Papa's Story 1

It's appropriate for all good stories to begin at the beginning. Thus, the Bible starts at the beginning of all things: the creation of the universe, the beginning of time, the beginning of all living plants, fish, birds, and other creatures, and the beginning of the human race. Every week, the parent and child should read over the relevant scripture as well as the Papa's Story.

Papa's Comments

Every parent should be acutely aware that their child is being aggressively indoctrinated into the world views of materialism. Atheism and evolution are the two main pillars of materialism. Public education, the news media, and every aspect of the current culture have embraced this worldview. Any Christian parent who is not actively and aggressively training their child how to deal with this barrage of false information is in serious danger of losing their child to this false religion (humanism).

At the end of my book, *Papa's Stories*, I detail a number of the reasons why the theistic/creationist worldview is the correct one and why the atheistic/evolutionist worldview is not.

The Bible is the Word of God, and it is truth. That includes the Creation Story, the Garden of Eden, the Fall of Man, the Flood, and God's Promise of Salvation.

Chapter 1
Discussion Points Questions

1. In Genesis 1, the phrase "According to its kind" is found ten times throughout the chapter. In the Hebrew language, repetition of a phrase is a literary method used to emphasize a particular point. Why do you think the author of Genesis (Moses, under the inspiration of God) emphasized this particular point?
2. In Genesis 1, the phrase "And God saw that it was good" is used six times. What is the author communicating to us?
3. After God had finished all the major acts of creation, in Genesis 1, verse 31, He looked at everything that He had created and He saw that it was very good. The Hebrew word for *very good* can be interpreted to be "perfect" or "complete." This was the end of day 6, and after that, it says that God rested.

Concluding Thoughts

1. Use your imagination and discuss what living in the garden would have been like for Adam and Eve.
2. Adam was given the task of naming the animals. Names have meanings, and in order to give an appropriate name, Adam would have had to closely observe an animal and learn something significant and unique about it. Have you ever named a pet? Was there a reason for the particular name that you gave it?
3. Adam and Eve seemed to know how to talk. Who do you think taught them to talk?
4. Do you think Adam and Eve had white skin? Or black? Or brown? Or yellow?
5. When Adam and Eve had children, what race do you think they were?

Advanced

1. In chapter 2, God created Eve from one of Adam's ribs. Knowing what we know today about DNA and genetics, what possible significance could that have?

Chapter 2

Paradise Lost

There Is No Fear in Paradise

Genesis 3
The Serpent's Trick
Disobedience Always Has Consequences
The Flaming Sword Protects the Tree of Life

"Are you kids ready for story 2?" Papa asked. "Do either of you remember what last week's story was all about?"

Lily asked, "Was it called 'The Beginning'?"

"That's right, Lily, and I asked you to use your imagination to think all the way back to before anything existed. No people, no animals, no plants, no earth, no sun, no sky, no days or nights—there wasn't anything, not even time.

"Then, with great care, God created a perfect place for the plants, animals, and people to live. Where on earth did his first man, Adam, live?" asked Papa.

"That's easy," replied Anna. "He put Adam in the Garden of Eden."

Papa continued, "Good. I also told you last week that man was created special. The Bible says that man was 'created in the image of GOD.' God created mankind so that He could have a personal and eternal relationship with them. God would watch over them and guide them and help them with all the details of their life, but He did ask for something in return. He asked them to trust Him and be obedient to the things that He asked of them. Even before God created Eve, God gave Adam a job. Do you know what one of the first things God asked Adam to do?"

"Yes," said Lily. "He asked Adam to name all the animals. We read the Bible in school every day. I learned it there."

"Naming the animals is actually a really big job. Names have meanings, and when Adam gave a name to an animal, the name was supposed to tell something that was unique about that animal. This meant that before Adam could name an animal, he first had to observe it and learn all kinds of interesting facts about it. After some time, I'm quite sure that Adam had learned many details about God's beautiful new creation. Adam and the animals lived in harmony. God provided for Adam and all the creatures, and there was peace everywhere. But something was missing.

God created Eve because, as He puts it, 'it is not good for man to be alone.'

"In addition to naming the animals, God gave Adam and Eve two responsibilities: 1) to care for and take personal responsibility for all of the creation and 2) to populate the earth with children and grandchildren."

Papa continued, "The Bible doesn't really tell us how long Adam and Eve lived in this perfect paradise called the Garden of Eden. They were both designed to live forever, and things like aging and death didn't affect them. Adam and Eve were perfectly free to enjoy God's beautiful creation in every conceivable way. However, as I said before, God did give Adam and Eve several responsibilities, and He expected them to obey Him. He warned them that the consequences of not obeying would be great. But his perfect creation wouldn't be perfect if man wasn't free. So God created man to be perfectly free. This meant that man even had the freedom to *not* obey."

The Serpent's Trick

"The Bible tells us that the garden was filled with every type of tree, plant, and grass that a person could ever desire. The story also says that there were two particular trees that God planted in the middle of the garden. One tree was called the Tree of Life, and the other tree was called the Tree of the Knowledge of Good and Evil. God gave Adam and Eve one very specific command. He told them, 'You may freely eat of the fruit of every tree in the garden, except the Tree of the Knowledge of Good and Evil. If you eat its fruit, you will surely die.'"

Papa continued, "The Bible tells us that there was one creature, the serpent, who was the shrewdest of all the animals that God had created. Among all of God's creatures, only the serpent had evil in his heart. The Serpent desired to ruin God's perfect creation. One day, the serpent, who was very attractive, approached Eve and asked, 'Did God really say that you must not eat the fruit from any of the trees in the garden?'

"'Of course we may eat from the trees in the garden,' Eve replied. 'It's only the fruit of the tree in the middle of the garden that we are not allowed to eat. God said if we do eat of that tree, we will die.'

"'You won't die!' the serpent lied. 'God knows that your eyes will be opened as soon as you eat it, and you will be like God, knowing both good and evil.'

"So what do you think Eve did?"

Lily quickly responded, "She ate the fruit, Papa. I know that from Sunday school. And then she gave some to Adam, and he ate it too."

Consequences for Disobedience

"I'm glad you know your Bible stories, Lily. So what do you think happened to Adam and Eve after they ate the fruit?"

Anna said, "I'm not really sure, but I don't think it was good."

"You're right about that, Anna. The first thing that happened was their eyes were opened, just like the serpent said. They did know, for the first time ever, disobedience. They already knew good. But now they knew both evil and good. And they were ashamed. They had never before disobeyed God, and for the first time ever, they felt shame. They wanted to hide, especially from God."

"Papa" said Lily, "couldn't Adam and Eve just tell God that they were sorry and He would forgive them?"

"Yes, they could. As a matter of fact, I'm sure that Adam and Eve were very sorry for what they had done. They had ruined their wonderful and close relationship with God, and all they got for it was shame and guilt. The serpent had certainly tricked them good. But even though they were really and truly sorry, there were still consequences."

"What do you mean, 'consequences'?" asked Anna.

"Let me explain it this way. Pretend that one day you were watching TV in your living room and your daddy came in and said that he wanted to watch West Virginia play football. You didn't like him telling you that he was going to take control of the TV, so you angrily threw the remote control at him—a little harder than you really meant to throw it. Unfortunately, your dad did not catch the remote, and it crashed right into the middle of your big TV screen, and glass sprayed all over the room as the TV fell apart. How would you feel?"

"Ashamed!"

"Would you be sorry?"

"Oh yeah, I'm sure I would be really sorry!"

"Would your mom and dad forgive you?"

"Probably not right away. They would be really, really mad!"

"I'm not sure they would ever forgive you for that, Anna," piped in Lily. "You know how much Dad loves that TV, and it cost a ton of money."

Papa smiled. "Anna, I know for sure that your dad would forgive you. But there would be several conditions for him to forgive you. First, he would have to know for sure that you were really sorry for what you had done. Second, he would probably make some rules for your behavior to make sure that in the future you have a lot better control over your anger and your actions. Do you think he would still love you?"

"I guess," Anna replied.

"I'm sure he would. But even though he still loved you the same, he still would probably do some things to punish you for what you had done. He would do those things to help you learn to control yourself better, not because he doesn't love you but because he does. But even after you asked them for forgiveness, and even after your mom and dad forgave you, there would still be a big problem."

"What's that?" asked Anna.

"You would still have a broken TV. Remember Lily's question a few minutes ago when she asked couldn't Adam and Eve just say that they were sorry and God would forgive them? The answer to that very good question is yes, they could ask for forgiveness and God would forgive them. But even after all that forgiveness, there would still be consequences. Earlier, God had warned them not to eat from that tree or they would surely die. God never lies, but the evil serpent did lie, and he fooled Eve. So what do you think the consequences were for Adam and Eve?"

"I'm not sure," Anna said. "They died?"

"They did die, Anna. But they didn't die right away. God had a plan so that one day his close and personal relationship with Adam and Eve could be completely restored. Facing the consequences for their disobedience would all be a part of their getting their relationship with God back to where it was at the beginning."

"So what did God do?" asked Lily.

The Consequences

"First, he told Adam that he and Eve would not have such an easy life as they had. From now on, if they wanted to eat, they would have to work real hard to grow food, and there would be weeds and water shortages and insects that would ruin the crops. Life would no longer be so easy. Second, having children would be a very difficult and painful experience. Third, they were banished from the Garden of Eden. God placed mighty cherubim to the east of the Garden of Eden, and he placed a flaming sword that flashed back and forth to guard the way back into the Garden and the Tree of Life.

"In order to have eternal life and have their relationship with God restored perfectly, the people had to eat of the Tree of Life, and the way back to that tree was through the flaming sword. As we continue with these stories, we'll learn more about that flaming sword. We'll also get to see how the serpent is a major character in the Bible story.

"So our next story, titled 'Outside of the Garden,' begins with Adam and Eve and their family living outside of the Garden of Eden."

Study Guide for Chapter 2 – Paradise Lost

Story 2: Paradise Lost
Read: Genesis 3 and Exodus 20:17
Read: Papa's Story 2

We all know the story of Eve eating the forbidden fruit and then Adam joining her in the disobedience.

Papa's Comments

Let's talk about "coveting." How true it is that we so often want the most the very thing that we are forbidden to have. We've all snuck a cookie out of the "forbidden" cookie jar when our Mama wasn't looking.

Coveting and jealousy are running rampant in the United States today. Many politicians get their power by enlisting hordes of our so-called poor people to support these elected officials. They are incessantly told that it is unfair that the rich people have things that they don't have. Promoting laws for redistributing the wealth has become the basis for many politicians to gain this very large and growing voting base.

It actually turns out that most poor people in the United States have automobiles, flat-screen color TVs with cable services, smartphones, high-speed Internet, and lots of other neat things. Most poor people in the United States, compared to the poor people in almost every other country, would be considered quite rich and fortunate. Yet many poor people in the USA are very, very unhappy. They're unhappy not so much because they are "poor" but because of the successful indoctrination of materialism.

The scriptures teach us that we should not covet, that we should be happy and satisfied with what we have and not be so obsessed with what other people have. Coveting other people's stuff can be the source of much unhappiness and misery.

Chapter 2: Discussion Points Questions

1. God gave names to two of the trees in the middle of the Garden of Eden. What were the two names? Which one was forbidden?
2. What did God say would happen to Adam and Eve if they ate from that tree?
3. At the end of Genesis 3, God says that Adam and Eve must be prevented from eating the fruit from the Tree of Life, for then they would live forever. So what did God do?
4. When Anna got angry and broke the TV, do you think she was sorry and ashamed for what she had done? Do you think her parents forgave her? But were there still consequences?
5. What were the consequences of Adam's and Eve's sin?
6. Remember the picture of the flaming sword. It is the key to getting back into the garden and to the Tree of Life.
7. Are you mad at Eve for sinning? Do you think that you would have been able to not sin? Does eating a piece of fruit seem so terrible to you? What was the *real* sin?

Concluding Thoughts/Questions

1. Before Adam and Eve sinned, they had no shame, they weren't afraid of anything, they had everything that they needed because God provided it, and life was really great. After they disobeyed God, there were consequences. They had shame, they had to go into a fearful world outside of the beautiful garden, and life was going to be really hard. Also, their bodies would begin to age and die. The consequences of their sin was really life-changing, and not for the better.
2. Did Anna sin against her dad or was her sin against God? She was certainly sorry for what she had done, and her dad did forgive her. However, there still were consequences from her angry action. What were the consequences?
3. When we sin, who are we sinning against, and what are the consequences?

Chapter 3

Outside of the Garden

Wild Animals Kill for Food

Genesis 3:16–24, Romans 3:23–25, Revelation 12:7–9
Food Is Scarce and Life Is Hard
Satan Leads the Whole World Astray
We've All Sinned like Eve

"Hi, Papa."
"Hi, Papa."
Anna and Lily walked into the living room.
"We're ready for the next story," Anna exclaimed.

"I'm glad, because I'm ready too," Papa said. "Do you remember what happened last week at the end of the story?"

"Adam and Eve were kicked out of the garden," Anna answered.

"Good, Anna. Do you remember why, Lily?"

"They ate the fruit that they weren't supposed to eat?"

"You remembered well, Lily. So now Adam and Eve found themselves outside of the Garden of Eden, and right away, they saw that things were a lot different than they had been in the garden. They noticed something else: they weren't the only ones outside of the garden. All of the animals had been banished as well. Apparently, what Adam and Eve had done had affected all of the creatures. And the land was totally different. They could only see a few trees, and they had to go a really long way just to find one scrawny apple tree.

"When they finally got to that apple tree, they saw that it only had several apples left on it because a bunch of hungry monkeys had gotten there first. When Adam reached up to pick one of the apples, a monkey screeched at Adam and reached out, and before Adam could react, the angry monkey had dug his fingernails into Adam's forearm, leaving a deep and painful scratch. Something like that had never happened before, and Adam was shocked.

"Before the day was out, it became obvious that gathering food was going to consume most of their time. They had to travel further and further looking for trees with fruit and some grasses with seeds that they could eat, and wherever they went, they found themselves fighting with the hungry animals. This was becoming a nightmare, but then Adam saw something that was even worse."

"What was that, Papa?" asked Lily.

"Adam was looking out over a field when he saw a group of giraffes eating the leaves off of some scrawny bushes that they had found. While Adam was looking, he saw a lion leap up from hiding in the bushes. After a couple of long running strides, the lion jumped through the air and landed on back of one of the giraffes. Then the lion bit down hard on the giraffe's neck. The frightened giraffe ran for a few steps, but it didn't take long before the giraffe fell down to his knees, and within several minutes, the giraffe stopped fighting.

"Then Adam saw and heard the most frightening thing he had ever experienced. The lion stepped back from the dead giraffe, lifted his head high to the sky, and, with his mouth stretched open to the limit, he made a deep roaring sound that echoed louder and louder for miles, and it seemed to go on forever. Never had Adam ever heard a sound so threatening. It seemed as if the whole world came to a stop as that awful sound swept over the land.

"After the sound ended and all the echoes had faded away, Adam saw the lion's family come out from the bushes, and soon, the six lions were all grouped over the fallen giraffe. It was clear to Adam that the lions were hungry and they needed food. The only food they could find was another animal. Of course, all of the other giraffes had run far away, and there would be no doubt that they would be watching out for hungry lions. Things had really changed in a hurry from the comfortable and safe life that Adam remembered in the garden.

"Adam and Eve travelled for several days looking for a good place where they could settle down. They needed to build some shelter, and they thought they would try to plant some trees and vegetables so that they wouldn't have to go hunting for food all of the time. They would have to protect their land and plants from the wild animals. As they walked, they came across three baby goats. It appeared that their parents had been killed and the babies were hungry and lost. Adam knew that if he and Eve would take care of these goats, the goats would one day have their own family and that they would be able to provide them with milk. So they gave the goats food and they protected them from wild animals.

"After several days, they came upon a stream flowing with cool, fresh water. The land seemed to have good soil that would support different plants and vegetables for a garden. There was a nice group of large shade trees nearby, and this looked like a good place to build a home. This surely wasn't the Garden of Eden, but if they were going to live, this would be a good place to start."

"This is a really sad story, Papa," Anna said. "Didn't God still love Adam and Eve?"

"He sure did love them, Anna, and God wanted to have the perfect relationship with Adam and Eve that they once shared every day in the garden. Remember when I told you that God knows everything? Even before God created the universe, and before even time began, God knew that Eve and Adam would disobey and sin. He wasn't happy about it, but He knew it would happen. In order to make Adam and Eve perfect, He had to give them perfect freedom. That meant that He had to allow them to make choices—even choices to obey or not obey.

"The Bible tells us that Satan was one of the most powerful angels in heaven. He was really smart, he was a leader, and he had great influence over other angels. Unfortunately, Satan wanted more than to just serve God. He wanted to be God and to act according to his own desires, not God's. Even though God is perfect and only has love for His creation, Satan is jealous, and he hates God. The Bible tells us that there was a great war in heaven and the great angel Michael and his angels fought against the dragon, who was Satan. Satan and his angels lost the war against Michael, and they were hurled down out of heaven and cast to the earth, where they now lead the whole world astray.

"God allowed this to happen, Anna and Lily. It was all a part of God's plan of salvation. Men would encounter the temptations of Satan, and they would all fail. Just like Eve, they would know evil. God, who loves his creation perfectly, cannot and will not have a relationship with evil. For men to have a relationship with God, they must reject evil and choose good. But man is sinful and incapable of making this change without help.

"The Old Testament is the story of how God provides sinful man with a way to do this. The way I put it, His plan of salvation provides sinful men with the opportunity to return to the Garden of Eden and live with God in paradise forever. Remember, the gate to the garden is protected by a flaming sword. The following stories will show how over a several-thousand-year period God uses special men, God forms a special nation, God inspires special prophets, and God causes incredible miracles, all in order to provide men with a chance to pass through the flaming sword and choose eternal life with Him. We will learn that this flaming sword is actually God's own Son.

"It's important that we are aware of Satan and how he can influence us. The Bible teaches us that Satan can take on different shapes, and he can be very attractive, even beautiful. We know that God always wants us to obey Him and do good things, to be kind to each other, to share, to look out for each other, to be helpful, and so on. What do you think Satan wants us to do?"

"He wants us to do the opposite," Anna answered. "Things like be mean, be selfish, to fight, and to disobey our parents."

"That was a great answer, Anna. Do you ever notice that Satan is having an influence on your behavior? Be honest now, this is a tough question."

Lilly couldn't wait. "Let me answer, Papa. The other day, Mommy asked me to pick up my room, but I really didn't want to. Anna was out jumping on the trampoline, and I wanted to go out there with her. So instead of picking up my room, I just snuck out past Mommy and jumped with Anna. Later, when Mommy asked me if I had cleaned my room, I said yes even though I hadn't done it. I was lying, but I figured that I could do it later and she would never know. But she already knew. She had been upstairs while Anna and I were jumping, and now I was in big trouble."

"So what happened?"

"Daddy spanked me. He said he was mostly upset with me for lying. I've never cried so hard before in my life. The spanking didn't hurt so much, but having Mommy and Daddy so disappointed in me was terrible."

"So where does Satan come into the story?"

We all waited patiently while Lily thought hard. Finally, she said, "When I had to decide whether to obey Mommy and pick up my room, or do what I wanted to do and go jump on the tramp, I think Satan might have helped me decide to disobey. Something made me think that I wouldn't get in trouble and that I could get away with it. I think that something might have been Satan."

"Does this remind you of the story of Eve and the Serpent in the garden?"

"Yeah, it kinda does."

"Now, let's get back to our story. In a way, Satan was telling Eve the truth when he told her that if she ate the forbidden fruit she would know both good and evil. She knew perfect goodness when she and Adam walked with God every day in the garden. After she and Adam sinned and they were kicked out of the garden, she saw evil all around her. She saw all kinds of fighting and death. She was always fearful of being attacked by a hungry family of animals. Life was so hard, and she knew hunger and pain, like she had never known in the garden. Most of all, she felt so separated from God. He seemed so far away. Unfortunately for Eve, she didn't really appreciate the perfect goodness of God until she knew evil.

"Many years went by, and Adam and Eve began a family. They got a lot better at growing food. They had learned how to plant and harvest crops and what kinds of trees and plants would grow in the different soils. They learned how to manage herds of goats and cattle. They still had the problem of protecting their property from the wild animals. They built walls and fences and made it difficult for animals to bother them. But life was still really hard, and Adam was noticing that after a hard day working in the field his knees would ache and he would have a hard time straightening up his back. If he ever got a cut or bruise, it seemed that it took longer to heal than when he was younger.

"He began to realize what God meant when He said, 'If you eat of this fruit that I have forbidden you, then you will surely die.' Even though Adam's body had been created to live forever, after he had been banished from the garden, something had changed, and very slowly, a little each day, his body was growing older and weaker. He knew that one day his body would totally stop working and he would die.

"In the evenings, Adam would gather Eve and his children and grandchildren around the fireplace and tell them stories, just like I'm telling you this story now. More and more, he found himself telling them about the garden and how wonderful life was there. Eve's eyes misted up just thinking about the wonderful times they had in the garden, and then she sighed and she looked so sad just thinking about all that had been lost. Adam told his family how great God was. But he also would tell them how serious disobedience was and the terrible consequences that happened when you disobeyed."

"I'm so mad at Eve, Papa," Anna cried out. "Why did she have to go and sin? She ruined it for all of us. It's not fair!"

"What exactly did Eve do, Anna?"

"She ate the forbidden fruit."

"Why did she do that?"

"Because the serpent tricked her."

"Very good. Have you ever done anything wrong because Satan tricked you?"

Anna thought hard for a minute. "I guess."

"Well then, you've sinned just as badly as Eve did. We've all disobeyed God, Anna. We've all been selfish and greedy and mean. We've all thought about ourselves instead of others. We've all let Satan influence our decisions. Remember when Lily lied about cleaning her room so that she could jump on the tramp with you? We shouldn't sit here and blame Eve for disobeying God. Every one of us would have done the same thing. The Bible has a verse that says, 'We've all sinned and fallen short of the glory of God.'

"Today's story was a sad one, but it's a true story, and we should know it well. We live outside the garden too. Just like Adam, there is something in me that longs for the garden. Wouldn't you love to go there?"

"Oh yes, Papa," Lily said. "But how can we go there? I thought that God had placed a flaming sword in front of the gate to keep people from just walking in."

"Well, Lily, that is what we'll be talking about in the next several stories. The next story is called 'God's Word to His People,' and it is the beginning of God's plan of salvation. This plan is what the rest of the Old Testament is all about."

Grammy got up and said, "Now if you two will promise to take your baths and get ready for bed, I might first have a little snack for you. I saw Papa put some chocolate ice cream in the freezer earlier today."

Study Guide for Chapter 3 – Outside of the Garden

Story 3: Life Outside the Garden
Read: Revelation 12:7–9, 2 Corinthians 11:11–15, 1 Peter 5:8
Read: Papa's Story 3

Papa's Comments

How life changed dramatically for Adam and Eve after they were banished from the Garden of Eden. Today's lesson provides a parent a great opportunity to talk about the reality of Satan. Every young child knows the internal war that takes place many times every day as they have to make hard decisions. Do I do what I *want* to do, or do I do what I *ought* to do? It's always *want* versus *ought*. Look at the mess that the world is in. This is Satan's kingdom.

These are difficult truths for a young child to understand, but they are true. Jesus was well aware of Satan's presence and influence in the world.

Imagine what life was like for Adam and Eve the day after they walked out of Paradise and into the wild world outside of the garden. They hadn't ever had to fight for their dinner. Never before had any animals threatened them. They were afraid, they were unsure of what to do, they were hungry, they were lost, but most of all, they were ashamed and sorry they had brought all this on themselves. At first, Adam and Eve wanted to blame the serpent who tricked them. He was really persuasive, and he did a good job of convincing them to disobey God. But they made the fatal decision, and now they were paying the price for their sin.

Review Revelation 12:7–9 with your child.

God created the angels, and they are spirits who serve God. However, one of God's angels, Satan, didn't like serving God. Satan wanted to be served, not to serve. Satan was a great deceiver, and he was able to convince a whole group of angels to follow him instead of simply obeying God. So just like how Adam and Eve were banished from the garden for their disobedience, God banished Satan and his followers. They were sent away from God's presence and to the same wilderness where Adam and Eve were sent. Planet Earth became Satan's kingdom, and he has great influence over the people there.

Satan is a spirit, and we cannot see him. But he is real. His spirit influences other spirits and is always trying to convince them to disobey God.

Chapter 3 Discussion Points Questions

1. Recall Lily's story about wanting to jump on the trampoline instead of cleaning up her room. She did what she *wanted* to do rather than what she *ought* to do. The consequences were not nice. She was ashamed, she got spanked, but most of all, she had disappointed her parents. After the whole incident was over and Lily could think about it, she came to the conclusion that it was Satan's spirit who had influenced her to disobey. Can you think of a time when you struggled with *want* versus *ought*? Do you think Satan might have been involved in that struggle?
2. Imagine a world where there was no fear of any other people or animals. What did you think of the story about the lion killing the giraffe? For the first time, Adam and Eve had to live with real fear for their safety. This new life outside of the garden was really bad. If you had been Adam or Eve, what would be the worst part? The shame, the fear, having to work so hard?
3. We live outside the garden too. Wouldn't you love to go back to the garden?

Concluding Thoughts

God knows everything. He knew that Eve would be tempted and that she and Adam would disobey. But God had a plan. Just like Adam longed for the garden and wanted more than anything to return, God also wanted Adam and Eve to come back. The remainder of the Bible is a long, long story of God's plan for His chosen people to find their way back to the garden and live together with Him in Paradise.

Chapter 4

God's Word to His People

Genesis 3:16–24, Romans 3:23–25
God's Perfect Plan
Adam Misses the Garden
Beware of the Serpent, He Deceives

"Dad, can you watch Anna and Lily for a couple of hours when we get back to your house?" Sally asked. "Mom and I have to go to the fabric store. Mom's going to help me make some new drapes for our living room, and we have to pick out the materials. The girls are looking forward to your next story."

"I'd love to watch the girls, but only if we have some ice cream in the freezer," Papa responded. "I can't stand Lily's constant begging for treats if we don't have chocolate ice cream. She's a worse beggar than our dog, Lucy."

"Don't worry. Mom and I will stop by Publix on the way home, and we'll take care of the Lily-begging problem."

Papa began his story. "Last week's story was titled 'Outside the Garden,' and it was a story of what life was like for Adam and Eve and all of the animals right after they had been banished from the Garden of Eden. The name of the next story is 'God's Word to His People.' What can you girls remember about the story last week?"

"It was a really sad story," Anna said. "It seemed like life was so hard, even for the animals."

Lily added, "The worst part was when the lion killed the giraffe. I don't think I'll ever forget how awful that was."

"Isn't that just the way it is today, Lily? Don't you think lions still kill other animals for food, even today?"

"I guess they do. I just don't like to think about it."

"Well, Adam hated it too. Adam and Eve both remembered what life had been like in the garden, and they hated this new life. Adam and Eve had learned that disobedience led to bad consequences, and they knew that because of disobedience they had given up an eternal life in paradise. We can only imagine how sorry they must have been."

Papa continued, "Not only was their life much more difficult, but there was death all around. It seemed that there was always a shortage of food. Sometimes, people would get sick, and even die. Animals were killing each other, and they would even kill people. All of God's creatures now had to live in constant fear. Life was indeed hard.

"Adam and Eve began raising a family, and they had sons and daughters. Cain, their first son, married Katherine, and they began a family of their own. They worked hard, and after many years, they became experts in growing all kinds of crops. People would come for miles around to learn from Cain and Katherine what their secrets were. As he grew older, Cain became quite famous and wealthy, and he took a lot of pride in his success.

"Abel, the second son, married Rose. Abel and Rose were interested in raising animals. Over the years, their goat herds and stables of horses grew to very large numbers. Just like Cain, Abel became famous throughout the land. Abel was recognized as an expert in raising animals.

"One day, Adam sent out word that he wanted his whole family to come together for an important visit. All of Adam's sons and daughters and their families responded to his invitation. After they had enjoyed a big family meal together, Adam gathered them all together and he said, 'Your mother and I have some very, very important things that we are going to tell you. I want you to repeat what I tell you to your children and teach your children to repeat these things to their children and so on, so that these important things will be known and remembered until the end of time. Please listen carefully because this is the most important story I can ever tell.'

"Kids, why didn't Adam just type up his story on his computer and e-mail a copy of it to all his children?"

Anna laughed. "You're crazy, Papa. You know Adam didn't have a computer, did he?"

"You're right, Anna. One, I am crazy, and two, computers hadn't been invented yet. In those days, the people would get together in big groups, and the older and wiser people would tell the less experienced what they had learned. These stories would be told over and over again, and this way, information could be passed down from parents to children and grandchildren and so on."

"Adam continued with his important story. 'Lately, your mother, Eve, and I have noticed how tired we get after working hard in the fields. We are beginning to understand that we are slowly dying. You have heard me speak many times about the garden and the wonderful life that Eve and I had living in paradise. We took walks every day in the garden. God's spirit spoke to us all day long and we had no fear, we never knew hunger or thirst, we lived in perfect harmony with each other and all the beautiful creatures. In the garden we never had any of these feelings that we were slowly dying.

"'Now that we have lived many years outside of the garden, it's becoming harder and harder for me to remember my life in the garden. I find myself crying out to God, begging Him to take me back to the garden. I want to go home because truly, I say to you, this difficult and fearful place is not home, I am just visiting here. My real home is in the Garden, and that's where I belong.'"

Beware of the Evil Spirit

Adam stopped talking and all eyes were fastened on him as he bowed his head and wept. After several long minutes, Adam looked up at his family and continued, "The other day, I was on my knees crying out to God, begging him to make His Spirit close to me again. I wanted that closeness, the way it was in the garden. I was so very sorry for my disobedience. I was also so aware of the serpent's spirit that is so powerful all over this world. Every day, I find that the spirit of that ancient serpent affects my thinking, and that evil spirit makes it harder and harder for me to sense the Spirit of my Father. I say to you, be aware the evil spirit is everywhere and is always trying to tempt you to disobey. The garden is God's wonderful domain, and this world outside the garden is the domain of Satan, the evil one. You have to be constantly on your guard. Satan comes in many shapes, and he always looks pleasing to the eye. He will use every method to tempt and trick you. Giving in to the serpent's temptation will always lead to separation from my Father, the one true God."

Adam's Vision: God's Perfect Plan

Then one night last week, after several hours of praying and crying out to God, I began to feel the wonderful closeness of His Spirit. It reminded me of walking in the garden so long ago. And God's Spirit began to speak to me. "Adam, I've missed you, my dear son. I created you for my own pleasure, and it breaks my heart that we aren't close like we once were. I know that you are now aware of the consequences of disobedience, and you're fully aware of the power of the evil spirit, who only desires to keep us apart. As you have learned, there is a high price for disobedience. You must teach this truth to your children. And they must teach this truth to their children."

I cried, "Oh, Father, why did you let Eve and me be so deceived by the serpent?"

Perfect Freedom Means We Can Sin

And He answered clearly. He said, "My perfect creation requires perfect freedom. Every person is given this perfect freedom, and each person will be deceived by the serpent, just like Eve and you were. Each person who sins will have to pay the consequences, which is separation from Me."

Then God, my Father, continued, "But of course, I, God, knew that this would happen, even before the beginning of time. Even before I created the world, I had a perfect plan for all of my people who desire to come back home to the garden. My perfect plan offers them a way back to Me and to the garden. My perfect plan is a free gift and is given to all those who desire to live in the garden with me forever. But each man must choose for himself to come home to the garden—or not. The serpent will always be doing his very best to deceive and to prevent men from making this choice. My creation enjoys perfect freedom, and this is a perfect plan. A great host of people will enjoy the garden with me for eternity, and they will be there with me because they accept my plan of salvation.

"Now, Adam," God continued. "I have just given you a short outline of my perfect plan, and there's much more to it. I will choose some of your descendants—men who have a heart for Me and yearn to know the truth. I will visit these men, just as I'm visiting you now. I will speak clearly to them, and they will add to My Word. These prophets will teach My Word faithfully to all the people who will listen. And some will listen, and many will not.

"When the time is just right, I will send my only Son, and He will be filled with My Spirit. He will come to the earth as a man, but My Spirit will always be in Him. He will teach men to understand My Word. His words are My Words, and His very life is My Word. At all times, My Son does My Will. The serpent will try hard to break

Him, but My Son will never fall to the temptations and tricks of My ancient foe. The whole world will be blessed through Him.

"My Son is my free gift to the world, and He will give His own life to pay for the sins of all those who repent of their sins and desire to come home to the garden forever. Adam, you must know how important it is for you to pass this truth on to your children and their children. My Word must be taught to all the people. Call all the elders together, and teach My Word perfectly to them so they can pass it on to all the people. Many people will have ears to hear and accept the truth of My Word, but many will not. It is not your job to make anyone believe, your job is just to pass My Word on and let each person decide for himself. Only I, the Creator God, will know their hearts.

"Now, Adam, there are several more things that you must teach your children and all the people. First, you must teach them your own story about the Garden of Eden. You must teach them about how wonderful and perfect your life in the garden was. Teach them about your wonderful relationship with Me and how we loved each other."

The Grand Gathering

"And second, it's really important to teach them about the serpent and how he deceives. The people have to be taught of the terrible, terrible consequences of sin. They need to know the awful price that must be paid for their disobedience. And in order to remind the people of this most important lesson, you will need to teach the people to hold a grand gathering every year. This will be a special time of remembrance, a time where My Word will be repeated to the people and they will all repent of their sins. Remember, there is a very costly price to be paid for sin.

"At this grand gathering, I will ask each person who has a repentant spirit, who is truly sorry for his disobedience to Me, to offer Me something of great value. I will know the hearts and spirits of the people as they make their offerings, and I will accept those offerings that come from a truly repentant spirit. Adam, go and teach the people well. My perfect plan begins with you."

Adam laid his head down on the table and fell fast asleep. His whole family sat quietly while Eve got up and put a soft pillow under Adam's head. Then the large family quietly got up and began returning to their homes.

Cain and Abel Disagree

As Adam's two sons walked along together, Abel said to his older brother, "Wasn't that an amazing story, Cain? Don't you wish we could visit the Garden of Eden to see what an incredible place that is?"

Cain stopped and looked at Abel like he was crazy. "Do you buy all this nonsense from Old Dad? He actually thinks that this God of his was his own father and that he and Mom actually lived in some garden where everything was perfect. He thinks we believe him when he says that there was no death and the lions were friends with the deer. He must have gotten hit over the head and his brains got all scrambled up. I've never seen such a place like that garden of his. Personally, I think he's nuts. I'm surprised Mom doesn't set him straight when he goes on like that. Then he tells us that we are being tricked by some serpent. Where does he come up with all this nonsense?"

"Well, brother" Abel replied, "I don't know about you, but I've often done things that I regretted, and I've wondered why. The idea that I was deceived by an evil spirit makes sense to me. I like Dad's story, and it explains a lot of things."

"Like what?"

"Like how we can draw closer to God. Like how we can also enjoy that wonderful garden that Dad always talks about. Like what happens to us after our body dies. I don't entirely get it, but I like Dad's story, and I can hardly wait for this Grand Celebration that Dad talked about."

"You're just as crazy as Dad, Abel. I sure hope Dad doesn't make me go to many more long drawn-out meetings like that. Well, goodbye, Abel, and good luck finding Dad's garden."

Cain and Abel parted and walked slowly back to their homes.

"Well, Anna and Lily, that is the end of today's story. Did you understand it okay?"

"I think so, Papa," Anna responded. "It's really an interesting story."

Lily chimed in, "Did you make all of this up, Papa?"

"The answer is yes and no. As you know, I've read the Bible a lot, and the Bible is God's Word to His People. I'm one of God's people, because I know that I have a heart that yearns to know God, the way Adam knew God in the garden. When you wanted me to tell you a story, I asked God to help me tell you about His Word, but to tell it in such a way that would be easier for you to understand. The Bible can be pretty difficult reading for little kids. It's even pretty hard for an old geezer like me. So every time I read the Bible, I first ask God to help me understand, and He does. And then, when I tell you a Bible story, I first ask God to help me tell it in a way that would please Him, and He helps me with that too."

Papa smiled at his two granddaughters. "I'm really proud of both of you for sitting there so long and listening so well."

"It's really fun to listen to you, Papa. And this is all starting to make sense. Can you tell us the next story soon?" asked Anna.

"Sure, Anna. Your mom asked me to pick you and Lily up after gymnastics next Thursday. The next story is titled 'Love and Hate.' Does next Thursday sound good?"

"Can we have ice cream first?" begged Lily.

Study Guide for Chapter 4 – God's Word to His People

Story 4: God's Word to His People
Read: Genesis 5
Read: Papa's Story 4

Papa's Overview on the Chapter

Papa's Story 4 contains a very good and understandable Gospel story (the Story of Salvation). A parent should take a good amount of time working through the key discussion points below. Hopefully, this chapter can be a real catalyst in your child's understanding and accepting the great salvation gift of God.

Review Genesis 5 with your child:

This list of people is known as the Line of Patriarchs. Many times in the Bible it is stated that even though a vast majority of men may reject God and His moral law, God has always kept alive a remnant of true believers in Him and His Word. Adam and Eve had a large number of children, but only Seth is specifically named in this list. Seth had numerous children, but only Enosh is named. This list continues all the way to the tenth generation, which was Noah's.

Noah was born about a thousand years after Seth. We have to remember how very long people lived at that time, and using a conservative geometric progression of population growth, there were most likely tens of millions of people on planet earth at the time of Noah. Later in these stories, when we read about Noah, we will learn that only Noah, of all the people on earth, was a true believer in God and His Word.

The Bible does not tell us exactly how God's Word was passed down from one generation to the next. This Papa's Story is just a possibility of how that happened. Remember, Papa's Stories are not inspired but are meant to teach biblical truths and stimulate discussion. It's important that parents explain this to their children. The Bible is inspired.

Spend time discussing with your child the following points:

- *Death.* In Genesis 3, God warned Adam and Eve that if they disobeyed, they would die. Then in Papa's Story 4, when Adam called his family together, he began by telling them that he was in the process of dying. Today, it is a well-known fact that everybody will, in fact, die. At least their earthly bodies will die. Christians believe that their souls will live forever with God, but everybody's body will age and die on this earth. Then in heaven, we will be given new bodies that will never die.
- *Satan's domain.* Then in Papa's Story 4, Adam went on to say that he was only a visitor to this place on earth and that his real home was with God in the garden. Likewise, when a person becomes a Christian, he/she becomes aware that this planet Earth is the domain of Satan. Christians are not of this world but are now citizens of the kingdom of God, which is in heaven (or the garden). We are aliens in a foreign and hostile land.
- *God's Spirit versus Satan's spirit.* Adam then went on to talk about the internal battle that his spirit was fighting every day. It is the battle of doing God's will or giving in to Satan's never-ending temptations to do my own will (which is always selfish and sinful). Admit to your child how Satan has influence in your own life. Ask your child if he/she is aware of Satan's influence over their thinking.
- *God uses man to teach His truth.* In this story, God tells Adam how important it is for him to pass His Word on to his children and grandchildren. God says, "My Word must be taught to all the people. Many people will have ears to hear and accept the truth of My Word, but many will not. It is *not* your job to make anyone believe, your job is just to pass My Word on and let each person decide for himself. Only, I the Creator, will know their hearts." Explain to your child that this is exactly why

you are spending this "most important" time with them today.
- *Perfect freedom.* This is an important theological concept. What would the world be like if we all "just obeyed God" and we always "did His Will," not because we wanted to but because He had made us like robots without the ability or capacity to disobey? Would we be free? Would our obedience be honoring to God? Spend some time with your child talking about the whole issue of freedom.
- *The prophets.* God tells Adam that His Word is incomplete and that in the years to come He will be giving special chosen men—prophets—special incites and truths. Eventually these truths will be written down. The Old Testament was written down over several thousand years and became known as the Word of God.
- God's Only Son: People often wonder how Old Testament people could be saved since Jesus Christ had not yet come to earth. Here, Papa conjectures that Adam understood the sacrifice that God would make on behalf of the human race. Theological experts seem to agree that Old Testament patriarchs and other true believers did have faith and were saved by that faith. We know that saving faith is faith in Jesus Christ, the Son of God, and the sacrifice that He made on our behalf. Somehow, these OT saints understood this. I believe that Adam understood and that he tried to pass this understanding down to future generations.

Final Comments

This is clearly the most significant chapter up to this point in *Papa's Stories*. The Old Testament salvation story continues as we go into the following stories. Chapter 4 really sets the stage.

Chapter 5

Love and Hate

Genesis 4
The Grand Gathering
Only a Few Believe the Word
Nonbelievers Resent the Believers

Anna Is Really Flexible

"Anna, I just can't believe how flexible you are," Papa said. "I can hardly touch my knees. That move you make where you put your hands straight up over your head and arch back, and you keep arching back until your hands are flat on the floor. Then you push back a little further, and the next thing you know, you've done a complete 360 and you're standing on your feet again. I just can't believe it. You ought to join the Cirque Du Soleil."

"You're funny, Papa. A lot of the kids on my team can do a back walkover. That's actually one of the easier moves that we have to make during our floor exercise."

"I don't know. It sure doesn't look easy to me. Not only that, but those other kids don't do that move nearly as effortlessly as you do. I still think you should concentrate on learning to stand on your hands for a really long time—perfectly straight and very still. I know judges really like that."

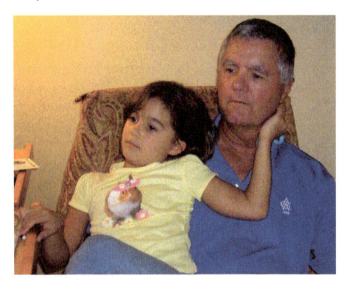

Twenty minutes later, the sisters were in their favorite positions, Anna on the couch with Lucy's head on her lap (Lucy is Grammy's and Papa's basset hound) and Papa in his easy chair with Lily on his lap.

Papa started, "Boy, that ice cream was good! Maybe ice cream is why I'm so fat. Before I begin this week's story, let's review last week's. The title last week was 'God's Word to His People.' Adam told a story to his family. Many of his children and grandchildren were at Adam's house when he told the story. Can you remember some of the things that he said?"

Anna answered, "Adam said that he and Eve really miss the garden. He said that the garden was his home and he hated his life here, that he was just visiting here and all he wanted was to go back to the garden where he belonged."

"That's a great answer, Anna. Do you remember anything from last week, Lily?"

"I remember two things. Adam said that the serpent is the ruler of this world and he is always trying to trick us into being bad. Then he said something about a Grand Gathering when all the people would come together. I can't remember what that had to do with the story."

"I'm impressed with both of your memories. At my age, I can hardly remember anything."

Papa continued, "Now, regarding that Grand Gathering, Adam wanted all the people to come together one day every year. This special day would be a Day of Remembering and Repentance. The Word that God spoke to Adam would be told to all the people. They would all be reminded about how the serpent is always working to deceive and there would be a time of repentance for sins and making offerings to God.

"Last week's story ended with two of Adam's sons walking back to their homes after Adam's long story. Cain, the older son, seemed to have a different reaction to Adam's story than Abel. Can you remember what they said to each other?"

"I don't think Cain believed his father," Anna answered.

"What didn't he believe, Anna?"

"He didn't believe that God was Adam's father, and he didn't believe in the serpent."

Lily added, "Cain thought Adam was crazy."

"So what did Abel think about Adam's story, Lily?" Papa asked.

"Abel believed Adam's story," replied Lily.

"Very good! That's enough review of last week's story. Now we're ready for a story of love and hate."

Several months passed by, and one day, Cain heard a loud ruckus outside his back door. When Cain ran into the backyard to see what was going on, he ran right into Abel. There were at least a dozen angry chickens running all around, flapping their wings and making all kinds of screeching sounds.

"What are all these screaming birds doing in my backyard?" Cain asked Abel.

"Well, Cain, last month when Rose and I visited you and Katherine for dinner, I noticed that your chicken coop had been visited by a fox, and it appeared that your flock was fairly skimpy. I don't have enough room for all the chickens Rose and I have been blessed with—we can't eat the eggs fast enough—and I'm more than happy to give you some from our surplus. You'll be doing me a favor by taking them off my hands."

"No thanks, brother. I'm not interested in your charity. Katherine and I are doing just fine, and if I need some chickens, I'll go to the market and purchase them. Now put them back on your cart, and be gone!"

"Please, Cain, I really want you to have—"

"No!" interrupted Cain. "Take them!"

"I'm sorry to have bothered you, Cain." Abel began gathering the chickens for the ride back., "Oh Cain, may Rose and I pick you and Katherine up on the way to Father's Grand Celebration next Friday? Rose and I are so excited about it."

"Oh, Dad's Grand Celebration. I almost forgot about it. Katherine and I won't be attending."

"Cain! You have to go. You know how important this is to Father. If for no other reason, go for the sake of Eve. She'll be so disappointed if her eldest son is a no-show, especially when it means so much to Dad."

"I'm only going to say this once, Abel, so listen carefully: Dad is crazy. All this stuff about his Father, the Creator God, the Garden of Eden, and the serpent is absolute craziness. For some weird reason, Abel, you have decided to believe it. Personally, I think you're nuts too, but you're my brother, so I'll give you some slack. But please don't expect me to buy into this. I'm way too intelligent for that.

"But I'll tell you what, Katherine and I will go to this big get-together for Mom's sake. Not because we want to hear any more of Dad's nonsense but for Mom. So Katherine and I will accept your offer to pick us up on the way to the event."

"Thanks, brother. Rose and I will be by at 2:00 p.m. next Friday."

So Abel went back home with his wagonload of chickens.

After several minutes, Cain went back into his house. His wife, Katherine said, "What was that all about? Was that Abel with all those chickens?"

"Yes, it was. Can you believe that he wanted to give us twelve chickens? How arrogant is that? Here's my little brother treating me as if I can't manage my own household!"

"Well, I think it was nice of Abel. He loves you, Cain. He's always looked up to you."

"He's crazy! He buys all that stuff that my dad has been spewing. But you and I both know that Dad is nuts."

"I'm not so sure, Cain. I wish you would listen with an open mind when Father speaks. Much of what he says makes sense to me."

"Katherine, I am the head of this household, and I will hear no more of this subject. Father is crazy! Abel is crazy! Anybody who listens to them is crazy! This is the end of this discussion!"

Friday arrived, and Abel and Rose pulled their wagon to a stop in front of Cain's house two minutes before 2:00 p.m. just as promised. In the back of their wagon was Abel's prize ram, the best male of Abel's excellent herd. After several evenings of praying and asking for God's forgiveness for his sins, Abel became convinced that only this particular ram would be a worthy offering.

"What in the world!" asked Cain as he and Katherine walked down the front walk to join Abel and Rose for the ride to Adam's Grand Gathering. "Do you expect us to go to this so-called Great Meeting with a beast in the wagon?"

"Relax, Cain," Abel said. "That beautiful ram is my sin offering. It took a long time and a lot of prayer for Rose and me to settle on the right offering."

"Offering? What are you talking about?"

"Cain, this ram is an offering, a payment to God. Rose and I are making this ram an offering to God for our sins. Hopefully, God will accept this sacrifice as an appropriate payment. What offering are you bringing?"

"I left it in the barn," said Cain. He jogged over to his barn and returned a minute later, carrying a bag filled with grain. After he tossed the bag in the back of the wagon, he told Abel, "Okay, we're all set to go now."

As they rode along on their way to the home of their parents, Cain's wife, Katherine, grew more and more upset. Finally, she couldn't contain herself anymore, and she pulled Cain to her and whispered in his ear, "That bag of grain is from the grain that was spoiled, and I know that you were already intending to burn it in the next several days. How in the world can you expect that offering to be an acceptable and worthy gift?"

"Hush, woman," Cain whispered furiously. "I am the head of this family, and what I offer is of no concern of yours. What's happening? Have you gone nuts just like Adam and Abel? Are you buying into all this nonsense of Adam's too? Everybody is going nuts! I can't stand it!"

Anna, Lily, and Papa all sat still for a few minutes and just thought about what was going on in this story.

"Lily, what do you notice about Cain?" asked Papa.

"It seems that he's mad at everybody."

"What about Abel?" asked Papa.

"Abel is really nice. He's trying to be nice to Cain, but it seems that the harder Abel tries to be nice, the angrier Cain gets. Now, Cain is even getting mad at his wife."

"What do you think is making Cain so mad, Anna?"

"I can't really figure that out. Abel and Rose and Katherine are only trying to be nice to Cain. Is Cain mad because they believe Adam's story and he doesn't? That doesn't seem like a good reason to get so angry," said Anna.

"Remember, Abel and Rose and Katherine are being influenced by God's Spirit and they believe in the Truth. Cain is being influenced by Satan's spirit and he believes in a Lie. Satan's spirit hates God's Spirit and he hates everybody who believes Truth. Do you understand?"

"I think so, Papa. This is kinda hard," replied Anna.

Abel and Cain and their wives arrived at the home of Adam and Eve shortly before dinner. The field to the east of the home was filled with dozens of wagons, and after a short time, Abel and Cain were able to find a good place to leave the wagon. After wiping down the horses and walking them to the stables, Cain joined up with the wives in Adam's large hall. Abel slowly walked his prize ram over to the holding pen, where many other excellent-looking animals were quietly grazing. Abel gave his ram a fond pat on the head and then turned and walked quickly away to join the others. The decision to offer that ram as a sin offering was difficult, but Abel was determined that God would honor his choice.

"Welcome, sons!" Adam said as he spotted his two elder sons and their wives on the far side of the hall. "Eve and I are always blessed to see our boys and their families! We love you both. Every day, I ask My Father to bless each of you and your families."

"Thanks, Dad. Rose and I pray for you and Mom every day as well," replied Abel.

"Excuse me Dad," said Cain. "I'd like to go and wash up before dinner. I got fairly soiled wiping down the horses after we arrived."

As Cain left the room, Adam pulled Abel aside and asked, "How's Cain doing? I feel a tension whenever I'm in his presence. Do you know anything? You know how much I love all of my children."

"I wish I could say that everything is fine with Cain, Dad. But ever since you revealed God's Word several months ago, Cain refuses to believe your stories about the garden. He says that it's ridiculous to think that your Father was the Creator of the universe. He thinks that anybody who accepts that idea is stupid. I hate to say it, but he thinks that you have lost your mind. The more I try to reason with him, the angrier he gets at me."

"How about you, Abel? Do you think that I've lost my mind?"

"Not at all, Dad. The more I think about this Word of God, the story that you told us, the more it makes sense to me. In addition, I am finding answers to many of the questions that I have struggled with over the years."

"What questions, Abel?"

"I understand how the evil spirit can influence me and tempt me to make a really bad decision. I understand that when I disobey God's will I always pay a price. Sin always has its consequences. Also,

I am starting to see myself as an alien in this land. Every day I find myself dreaming about my real home in the garden. I don't doubt you, Dad. I'm sure that your story about your Father and the garden is true. I only wish that my brother, Cain, could see things as I do. What can I do?"

"Pray for your brother, Abel. Whether or not Cain will believe is in the hands of my Father. All you can do is love him as a brother. You and Rose should pray for Cain every day."

"Thanks, Dad. We'll do that."

By sundown, the family had gathered for a great dinner. Afterward, everybody listened carefully as Adam and Eve shared stories about the garden and their great love for their Father.

After several hours, Adam stood up and said, "We've had enough stories of the wonderful garden. Now it is time for us to face the reality of our own existence out here, outside of the garden. I know for sure that each of us has felt the influence of Satan. He is everywhere and never gives up trying to get us to sin against the will of my Father. If we are honest, we will all admit that the serpent has had victory over us many times. We are separated from my Father's Spirit because we give in to the serpent.

"To feel the wonderful closeness of God's Spirit, we must be forgiven of our sins. In order to be forgiven, we must be truly repentant, and then we must ask God for forgiveness. If we want to be forgiven, we must also have forgiving hearts. Our relationships with our fellow men are very important to my Father.

"Lastly, as a token of our repentance, God requests a sacrificial offering. He knows our hearts and will accept the offerings of truly repentant souls. As we make our sincere offerings, God's Spirit will fill us with joy and satisfaction. We will know that we are loved, and we will be able to enjoy our God forever."

Adam then said to his family, "It is now time for each of us to make our special offering to the Father." He led the whole group outside to where a great stone altar had been prepared.

Adam said, "Now, dear Father, with repentant hearts, we are sorry for all of those times when we have gone astray and we've done what we know is wrong. We now ask you to accept our sacrificial offerings."

Each person laid his sin offering on the altar. Adam and Abel slew the live animals with their knives. After all the offerings had been arranged, Adam carried a burning torch to the wood that had been placed beneath the altar and lit the fire. As the fire burned and the offerings were consumed, all the people fell to their knees, and their hearts were laid bare before the Creator God.

As Adam looked over his family and sensed the sincerity of their prayers, he made eye contact with his eldest son, Cain. Cain was standing back, away from the group, glaring at Adam with a look of disgust. As Adam watched, Cain turned and walked away from the gathering and back to the stables. He obviously wanted nothing to do with this worship service.

About an hour later, Abel, Rose, and Katherine were leaving the big celebration and looking for Cain. It was getting late, and they had to get back home. Suddenly, Cain appeared, driving the wagon. As he pulled up to a stop, he said, "Hurry up, we've got to leave now. Dad's Big Meeting is over, and it's time for us to go home."

Now the end of this story is really quite sad. Three days after they had returned home from the celebration, Abel was out in his pasture fixing a broken-down fence. He looked up as he heard a sound, and seeing the face of Cain, Abel smiled and began to say, "Hello, brother, it's good to—"

But Abel never finished that sentence. Without warning, and before Abel could react, Cain swung a hammer in a wide arc and hit Abel square in the forehead. Abel died instantly while Cain stood over him triumphantly. Minutes passed, and Cain was overcome with shame and guilt. He took Abel's shovel and quickly dug a shallow grave and buried Abel. Then he did his best to cover up the evidence of this murder. As Cain left the field, he was filled with a dread, unlike any dread he had ever felt before.

"Anna and Lily, how are you two doing with this story?"

"What happened to Cain, Papa?" asked Anna.

"As Cain neared his own home, he felt a powerful and awesome presence, and he couldn't move. He knew that he was in the very presence of God, and that God was not pleased."

"Where is your brother, Abel?" asked God.

"How would I know? Am I my brother's keeper?" replied Cain with a shaky voice.

"You do know, Cain! Do you think that I don't see everything? The very ground that you stand on cries out for what you have done. Abel loved you, Cain. For doing this hateful thing against your brother who loved you, you will be banished from this land, and you will have to live in a far-off land, where life will be very hard. Your crops will fail year after year. You will no longer be an heir to your father, Adam."

Papa paused and looked at his beautiful little granddaughters for about a minute.

Finally, Lily asked, "Why did Cain hate Abel so much, Papa?"

"That's a really interesting question. The same thing happens today. Until a person becomes convinced in his heart that God's Word is Truth, he or she will be deceived by Satan, even if they are not aware of it. Satan hates God with all his heart, and he will try to influence the nonbelievers to hate the believers, even when there is no reason for them to hate. Many Christians have been persecuted throughout history for no other reason than they believed God's Word. This persecution is even happening all over the world today. It's not as bad in the United States as it is in many other countries, but it is getting worse here every day.

"The Bible says that God's Spirit is at war with Satan's spirit and that this is the reason that believers are always in conflict with nonbelievers. We'll see this conflict over and over as we continue with these stories. Next week's story will be a familiar story that you both know well. It's called 'The Flood.'

"Now I'm going to ask you two to pick up the ice cream bowls and rinse them off before putting them in the dishwasher. Then let's surprise your Grammy by picking up this messy living room before she comes back with your mother."

"We didn't make this big mess, it was Courtney and Ashley from earlier today," complained Lily.

"Grammy didn't make that mess either. How many messes of yours do you think Grammy picked up when you were little, like Courtney and Ashley? Are you listening to God's Spirit right now, Lily, or the Serpent's spirit?"

"Come on, Lily, let's pick up this mess before Grammy gets here," said Anna.

Study Guide for Chapter 5 – Love and Hate

Story #5: Cain and Abel
Read: Genesis 4
Read: Papa's Story 5

Papa's Comments about the Story of Cain and Abel

This is a well-known Bible story. Unfortunately, the actual Bible story about Cain and Abel is only several verses long, and consequently, we know very little about these two sons of Adam. In expanding this story, Papa tries to explain why Abel's sacrificial offering was accepted by God while Cain's offering was not. Papa also attempts to explain what made Cain so upset that he murdered his brother.

We have to remember that Papa's story about Cain and Abel is not actual Bible teaching; it is only speculation. Papa is trying to get the reader to think about what God looks for in a sacrifice. Papa wants to stimulate discussion on this important subject.

About sacrifice: Review the following paragraphs with your child.

While living in the garden, no sacrifice was ever necessary as a sin offering. Adam and Eve lived in perfect harmony with God. Then they disobeyed and were banished from God's presence and the perfect life in the garden. Isn't it interesting that the very first chapter in the Bible after Adam and Eve are banished from the Garden of Eden involves sacrifice? The Bible says that both Cain and Abel brought offerings to be sin sacrifices to the Lord. Obviously, God taught Adam and Eve that true repentance and a worthy sacrifice is what is required as a payment for their sins. Adam and Eve taught this to their family.

God is really serious about sin. He hates it when we sin. We are taught that in order to make ourselves right with God we have to truly repent (turn away) from our sin, and as a symbol of our repentance, God requires us to offer to Him something of great value to us. Throughout the Old Testament, we see this over and over again.

Abraham, Isaac, Jacob, Moses, Joshua, the prophet Samuel, the prophet Elijah, King David, and many more men of God made sacrifices for their own sins and for the sins of the people of Israel. These sacrifices were always meant to be costly, and they always had to be offered with a sincerely repentant heart, or God would not accept the sacrifice as worthy.

The Bible says that God accepted Abel's sacrifice but not Cain's. Most likely, Abel had faith in God and was truly repentant for his sin. Abel sincerely desired a close relationship with God. Cain, on the other hand, only made his sacrifice out of a sense of duty. He had been taught by Adam that this was something that he should do. Cain didn't really believe in God, nor did he desire to have a close relationship with Him. He was not truly repentant for his sins, and consequently, God did not accept his sacrificial offering as worthy.

Satan is real. We live in Satan's domain, and only by submitting ourselves to God can we successfully fight off the influence that Satan will have on us. Satan hates God, and so Cain, who was under the influence of Satan, hated his brother, Abel, who trusted in God.

This story brings up a number of theological issues:

- Why God requires sacrifice for our sins
- What constitutes a "worthy" sacrifice
- How pride can prevent a person from finding the truth
- Why Cain hated Abel
- How this hate is related to Christian persecution

Questions to Discuss:

1. Describe the attitude that Abel had toward Cain.
2. Describe the attitude that Cain had toward Abel.
3. Why wouldn't Cain accept the offer of chickens that Abel made? What was Cain's problem?
4. What should your attitude be toward a person who doesn't agree with you on important issues like these?
5. When God confronted Cain after he had murdered his brother, Cain asked, "Am I my brother's keeper?" How would you answer the question? Are you your brother's keeper?
6. Do you understand why God accepted Abel's offering and not Cain's? What does repentance have to do with it? Do you think the fact that Abel offered a prize ram and Cain offered a bag of grain had anything to do with God not accepting Cain's offering?
7. Is God more interested in your sacrifice, or is he more interested in your heart? How does obedience fit into this discussion?
8. If God is really just interested in your heart, what is the purpose of sacrifice?

Chapter 6

The Flood

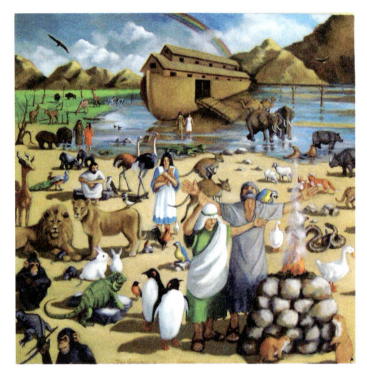

The Human Race Starts Over

Genesis 6–9
Only One Man Is Righteous
Noah Is Faithful and Obeys God

"I love Thanksgiving, Grammy!" said Lily. "You make the best mashed potatoes. I like them with lots of butter and a little salt. But I don't like gravy."

"Thanks, Lily," replied Grammy. "But it was your daddy who made the mashed potatoes and your aunt Lena made that bean casserole that I saw you wolfing down."

"Thanksgiving is one of my favorite days too," said Papa. "When the whole family gathers together—"

Anna interrupted, "Hey, Papa, this reminds me of the time when Adam called all of his family together. It was called the Grand Gathering. He told his family a story. You promised Lily and me another story today, so why don't we have a Grand Gathering of our family?"

"That sounds like a grand idea, Anna," Papa said. "I have to give all of you a quick update on the previous stories. This story, 'The Flood,' is actually the sixth story in my series. 'The Beginning,' the first story, was about the Creation of the universe, first the stars and planets, then preparing this earth, then the plants, the fish, the birds, the animals, and finally man. Then God created Eve to be a wife to the first man, Adam. They lived in a perfect place called the Garden of Eden. Everything was peaceful and good, the animals were all friends, and there was lots of food. The Garden of Eden is what I imagine heaven will be like.

"The second story was called 'Paradise Lost.' What happened in that story, Lily?"

"Eve ate the forbidden fruit, and then Adam ate it too."

"Why, Anna?"

"The serpent told her that she wouldn't die, and she really wanted that particular fruit."

"Very good, but why did she want that particular fruit?"

"She wanted it because it was forbidden, and she let Satan convince her that God wasn't telling her the truth. It seems that we always want the things we can't have," answered Anna.

"So true. What happened to Adam and Eve, Lily?" asked Papa.

"They were kicked out of the garden."

Anna added, "And they began to die, and all the animals were kicked out too."

"You remember well. The next story, 'Outside of the Garden,' was a story of what life was like for Adam and Eve right after they left that perfect life. Life was no longer so perfect. It was really hard to find food, and all the animals were fighting over the little that they did find. The animals would even attack Adam and Eve. Finally, Adam and Eve built a home and some fences for protection, and they began to raise a family.

"Then I told a story called 'My Word to My People.' Adam called a Grand Gathering of his whole family. He told them all about the life that he and Eve had lived in the garden, and how he wanted to go back there. He said that this was not his home, that the garden was his home. He told them to pass this story on to all the people, because it is the most important story they could ever hear. He told them that the spirit of Satan, who tricked Eve in the garden, is all over this world tricking people all the time. Satan hates God and will do anything that he can to keep people from believing and obeying God.

"Last week's story was about two of Adam's sons, Cain and Abel. Abel believed the stories about the garden and about God being the Creator of all things, including Adam. And he believed Adam's story about the serpent. Cain, on the other hand, did not believe. He thought that Adam was crazy. Cain had never in his life seen anything that resembled this garden of Adam's imagination. As this story progressed, Cain got angrier and angrier with Adam and Abel, and everybody else who listened to Adam. This story ends with Cain getting so mad that he killed his brother, Abel. God confronts Cain and banishes him from the land.

"Now we're ready for story number 6, 'The Flood.' Hundreds of years have passed since Cain killed Abel. For many years, Adam called his family together for the Grand Gathering. Adam would tell stories about the garden, and then the people would make sacrifices as sin offerings. But slowly, over the years, fewer and fewer people would show up for these gatherings. Then one year, Seth and his family were the only ones to show up for the celebration. Seth was

Adam's third son. Everyone else had an excuse. Like Cain, most of the people felt that Adam had lost his mind.

"Finally, Adam died, and only Seth, of all of Adam's many sons, attended the funeral of Adam. Standing over Adam's grave Seth made this promise: 'Father, I'm sorry that so many have not believed you. I know in my heart that your story about God, who was the Creator of all things, is truth. I can feel the power of Satan's Spirit sweeping over this land, and I have to fight hard every day to allow God's Spirit to be my spirit. I promise that I will continue, to the best of my ability, to pass on the Word to my children, and I will encourage them, as you did me, to pass the Word on to their children.'

"Seth stayed true to his promise. Seth had many children, and year after year, Seth would call all of his family together and repeat the words that Adam had taught him. They would hold a Grand Gathering and offer sacrifices for their sins. But eventually, only one son, Enosh, believed. Enosh, like Seth passed the Word down to his family, but only Kenan believed. Thus, as the world was filled up with more and more people, only a very small number of Adam's descendants believed the Word that Adam received from God Himself so many years before. The nonbelievers were not aware of it, but they all believed in the lies of the serpent.

"The Bible says that God looked down and saw how great man's wickedness had become. The thoughts of men's hearts were evil all of the time. The Lord was grieved that He had made man. So the Lord said, 'I will wipe mankind, whom I have created, from the face of the earth, the men and the animals...I am grieved that I have made them.'

"What happened then? Do you remember from Sunday school, Lily?"

"God decided to save Noah," Lily replied.

"Very good, Lily! Only Noah, of all the people on earth, was a believer in the Truth, and God decided to save Noah and his family.

"Noah lived in an area where water flowed from springs and streams, but there were no big lakes or oceans. God asked Noah to do something really strange. He gave Noah very detailed instructions to build a huge ship, a ship unlike any that the world had ever seen before. This boat was so big that it would take Noah and his family many, many years to build it. It was built on dry land, far away from any lake or ocean. Of course, the neighboring people thought that Noah had completely lost his mind. Noah and his family became the laughingstock of the area.

"But Noah believed God, and he continued to build the ship. Many times over the long years, Noah felt the evil spirit of the serpent tempting him to quit. Satan tried to convince him that the people were right, and that this ark thing was just a big waste of time. And from time to time, Noah would begin to doubt, but because he was a disciplined man of faith, he would spend time before God on his knees, and God would always encourage him to continue.

"One hundred years passed by. Imagine that, one hundred years! Then one day, when Noah and his eldest sons, Shem and Ham, were finishing up the final coat of waterproofing, Japheth, Noah's youngest son, ran to the ark, shouting, 'Father, Shem, Ham, look! Can you see it?' He was pointing out across the large meadow.

"What in the world!" exclaimed Noah. "Is that giant beast a giraffe? Are those two baby elephants? Can that be a lion cub sitting on the back of that zebra? I've never seen anything like it. I think God is calling these animals to the ark."

For several days, the meadow filled up with hundreds of wild animals. Noah and his sons were as amazed as the townspeople. Only Noah understood what was happening. Each day, Noah would stand on the top of his ark and speak out loudly to the people, inviting them to repent of their sins and join Noah and his family in the ark. The more Noah spoke, the angrier and more hostile the people became. They were offended that this crazy old man would be preaching to them and telling them how they should live.

Once again, Noah's son Japheth ran to the ark, shouting, "Father, Ham, Shem. The giant giraffe just had two baby giraffes. They're right over there in the field."

Noah shook his head and, with a smile on his face, said, "That explains it."

"Explains what, Father?"

"Nowhere on the ark do we have a pen large enough for that giant giraffe. But those two small giraffes will fit nicely. Now Ham, Shem, and Japheth, tonight I want each of you to take your wives and children onto the ark."

"What about all the animals, Father?" asked Shem.

"Even now God is leading them to the ark," answered Noah.

All heads turned toward the ark, and sure enough, the animals were quietly forming a long line right in front of the main gate to the ark.

Noah said, "Hurry now, and gather your families. Your mother and I will go ahead and open the gate. We'll start letting the animals on and into their pens."

It was an amazing sight. When Noah opened the gate, the animals began walking in a very orderly fashion up the walkway and into the ark. Not only that, but each animal seemed to know which pen was designed just for him. By the time Noah's sons returned with their families, all the animals were on board and settled. Then before Noah closed up the gate, he looked out over the countryside. He wanted to make one more offer to the townspeople to repent and join him and his family on the ark. But all the townspeople had gone home.

For seven days, Noah, his family, and all the animals lived on the ark, and there was no sign of water. The townspeople would stop by and yell at Noah and his family. "You're a crazy old fool, Noah! Where is this God of yours now? How long are you going to stay on that old boat with all those wild animals?"

But then on the morning of the eighth day, there was a deep rumbling. The whole world shook slightly, and then it began. At first, a small stream of water began flowing down the hill. Then after a short time, that stream was joined by another and then another. Soon the waters were rushing from all directions upon the ark. The sky turned black, and it began to rain. The waters from below were coming up and joining the rains from above. It rained and rained, harder and harder. When it seemed that it couldn't possibly rain any harder, it would rain harder still. Then a terrible thing happened.

"What was that, Papa?" asked Lily.

Noah and his family heard the townspeople screaming and shouting. They heard a clear voice say, "Noah, we demand that you open up that gate and let us on the ark."

But Noah and his family sat still.

"Why didn't Noah let the people on, Papa?" asked Anna. "I thought you said that he had invited them on many times."

"That's a good question, Anna. Noah had always asked the people to repent of their sins, and then they would be welcome to join him and his family on the ark. These demands of the people facing the floodwaters were not the demands of a repentant group of people. No, Noah would not let this group of angry enemies of God onto the ark."

The Bible says that the earth continued to groan and shake like never before, and the waters kept rising until every mountain was completely covered. All of the people and the animals, except for those on the ark, perished. The rain and the flood continued for forty days and nights, and then it stopped. Even though the ark was tossed around on the turbulent water, the design of the ark was perfect, and all the animals and all of Noah's family survived the ordeal.

The water covered the entire earth for 150 days. Finally, it had receded enough, and the ark settled on dry land, near the top of a high mountain. As soon as Noah led his family off the ark, they built an altar and made a sin offering to God. And God made a promise to Noah.

"I know," Anna said. "God promised that He would never flood the world like that again. And then He put a rainbow in the sky. He said that the rainbow would be a sign of that promise."

"That's right, Anna. Every time you see a rainbow, you should think of God's promise and the story of Noah."

Papa continued the story.

Now Noah and his family would have to start building the human race up all over again. Imagine the entire population of the whole world is reduced to this one small family.

Remember the story of Adam? Even after Adam and Eve were banished from the Garden of Eden, they could still remember what that perfect life was like in the garden. In the same way, Noah could still remember what life was like before the flood. He could remember how very evil the people had become. Noah understood how Satan dominated the hearts and minds of the vast majority of the people. Now that he had been saved from that life, he was determined that he would teach God's Word to his children and that they would know the truth. They had to be aware of the evil spirit who was still working hard every day to deceive Noah and his family.

Eat Meat and Have Shorter Lives

There are two other things that the Word of God teaches us at this point. God told Noah and his sons that all the animals would be theirs for food. Until then, men did not eat the meat of animals, they were vegetarians. Also, God said that it is not so good that men live such long lives. Before the flood, it was normal for a person to live well over five hundred, sometimes even over nine hundred, years. God saw how evil a man could become when he lived that long. God changed things so that in the future man would die much younger.

Now God would begin a long process of completing His promise. His Word, which was His revelation to His people, would be written down by special men who would be inspired by God. He would begin this process by forming a special nation of people—people to whom God would reveal much about himself. This plan would take over two thousand years to complete.

Papa looked at his family said, "This Grand Gathering of the Marcus Clan was a nice idea. You're all welcome to join Anna and Lily and me whenever you can. I've been writing these stories down so that each of you can have a copy and teach them to your children. Then one day, your children can teach these stories to their children, and so on. Remember, this is the most important story that I can ever tell you. Always be aware of the spirit of the serpent. He will do everything he can to deceive you and to keep you from knowing the truth."

Study Guide for Chapter 6 – The Flood

Story 6: The Flood
Read: Genesis 6–9, Luke 3:23–38
Read: Papa's Story 6

Papa's Comments about the Story of Noah and the Flood

This is another well-known Bible story. Papa begins this story talking about how the Word passed down through the generations from one patriarch (believer) to the next patriarch. Papa's story indicates that only a very small percentage of the descendants would believe the Word of God. The Bible does teach that by the time of Noah, there was only one true believer on earth.

Spiritual Truths in This Story

Review these concepts with your child:

- God is really serious about sin.
- Noah had to trust God for a really long time. Trusting God may involve patience, perseverance, ridicule, and even persecution.
- Didn't you love the part of the story where all the animals line up and go onto the ark? Would you call this a miracle? God is in control of the animals too.

Questions to Discuss:

1. When it started to rain, the people demanded that Noah open up the ark doors. Why didn't Noah let the people on?
2. It took Noah a hundred years to build the ark. There were no lakes or oceans anywhere around where he was building the ark. The townspeople must have thought he was totally crazy. What are some of the Christian attributes that Noah demonstrated?

3. What was the first thing that Noah did once he was able to leave the ark and step on land? Did Noah understand how serious God is about man's sin?

Noah is one of the Patriarchs. That means that he was one of Adam's descendants who understood and believed in God's plan of salvation.

Review Luke 3:23–38 (the ancestors of Jesus).

After Noah, God's Word was passed down to the next generation through Noah's son, Shem. However, it wasn't long before most people did not believe, and the world soon began to look a lot like it did before the flood. But God had made a promise to Noah.

1. What promise did God make?
2. What sign did God give to Noah regarding this promise?
3. What should we remember whenever we see a rainbow?

Two other interesting things to note about this story:

1. Review Genesis 6:1–3. Note that God decided that men should not live so long. After the flood, God would begin a process of making the number of years that man could live on this planet considerable shorter. Why didn't God want men to live so long?
2. Read Genesis 11:10–26. This chapter is a list of Shem's descendants. Note how in just several generations people were not living such long lives.
3. Read Genesis 9:1–4. Ever since the creation of the world, man was a vegetarian. Now after the flood, God told Noah that eating the meat of animals was acceptable.

Chapter 7

Obeying God's Promise

Genesis 12–24
God's Promise to Abraham
Abraham's Obedience
The Big Ideas in the Bible

Abraham Obeys God

"Well, Anna, I guess this next story is just for you and Lily again," Papa said. "That Grand Gathering of the Marcus Clan last week was fun, wasn't it?"

"Ya, I really like it when the whole family is all together, Papa," said Lily. "Before you ask, this week's story is called 'Obeying God.' I remembered! That means we get ice cream after the story." She spoke with authority.

"You drive a tough bargain, Lily. But okay." Papa smiled at Lily. "With all that ice cream, how do you stay so skinny?"

Lily jumped up on Papa's lap while Anna decided to sit in Grammy's easy chair.

Papa began, "We ended last week with Noah and his family and all the animals getting off of the ark near the top of a high mountain. The floodwaters slowly receded, and Noah's sons and their wives begin the human race all over again. They had just experienced the incredible flood, and they were saved from this terrible worldwide punishment because Noah trusted God. Wouldn't you think that his family would all be true believers? Wouldn't they teach God's Word to their children?"

Anna agreed, "After all that, I would believe God."

"Do you think that God was pretty serious about sin?" Papa asked.

Lily replied, "I'd say that He was. He killed the whole world."

"Do you remember what I said about Satan and his evil spirit?"

Anna answered, "He survived the flood too."

That's right. Satan was still working hard to deceive the people. The Bible tells us that Noah's sons—Shem, Ham, and Japheth—all moved away in different directions and began to have lots of children. Even though they tried hard to teach God's Word to their families, Satan's spirit was strong, and before long, only a small number of the people believed. The world was, once again, starting to look like it did before God caused the flood.

Remember, God knows everything, and even before He created the world, He knew that the people would be tempted by Satan's deceptions and lies and that most of the people would reject the truth. But God had made a plan so that people could be saved. God still wanted His people to be drawn back to the garden and eat of the Tree of Life and live with Him forever. But remember, before they could get back into the garden, they had to pass through the flaming sword. God's plan was to show people the way through the flaming sword.

God's Plan Requires a Chosen Nation

In those days, the believing fathers would teach their children God's Word, and then, in turn, those children would teach their children. But God's Word still was not complete. There were many more things that God had to teach the people.

The next step in God's plan was to form a special group of people—a special chosen nation. His plan would take several thousand years to finish, and it would begin with just one man, a man called Abram. Abram was one of Shem's (Noah's son) great-great-great-grandsons, and he lived in a city called Ur. If Ur was still standing today, and it is not, it would be about a hundred miles north of Bagdad, in Iraq, several hundred miles east of Canaan, which is now Israel.

The Command and the Promise (Gen. 12:1–3)

The Lord said to Abram, "Leave your country, your people, and your father's household and go to the land I will show you. I will make you into a great nation, and I will bless you. I will make your name great, and you will be a blessing. I will bless those who bless you, and whoever curses you I will curse; and all the peoples on earth will be blessed through you."

It's really important for us to understand this promise and what God was asking Abram to do. The Bible says that Abram was seventy-five years old when God called him. He had a wife, Sarai, but they had no children. In those days, it was very dangerous to travel, and he was being asked to leave his safe home and travel to a strange place where the cities were walled and the people hated strangers. What God meant when He said "I will make you into a great nation" was if Abram would trust God and obey His commands, he would have children and his descendants would form a great nation. This nation of Abram's descendants would be a part of God's plan to bring salvation to this lost world. In other words, God would show people the way back to the garden.

Abram was a believer. He trusted God, and he obeyed. The Bible says that he took his wife, and with all their possessions, they went to the land of Canaan. Obeying God could not have been an easy thing for Abram to do. He was being asked to leave a safe place and familiar surroundings and move off to a dangerous and unknown land.

God told Abram that this far-off land was the Promised Land. Times were tough, it was difficult getting food, the people of Canaan were hostile, but God watched over Abram and Sarai and kept them safe. But they never had any children, and the years were passing by. Abram and Sarai were getting very old and had passed the time when people normally had children. Abram began to doubt that God would keep up His part of the bargain and that he would never have a child. How could he be the father of a great nation if he and his wife, Sarai, never had a son?

More years went by, and still, Abram and Sarai were without a son. Finally, when Abram turned one hundred and Sarai turned ninety, Sarai had the promised child. They named him Isaac.

Anna raised her hand, and Papa stopped. "Why does it say Abram was too old? Wasn't Noah five hundred years old when God asked him to build the ark?"

Papa nodded approval at Anna and said, "The Bible says that before the flood, God saw how evil man could become and that it wasn't good to allow men to live such long lives. At the end of the story last week, I mentioned that God would no longer allow men to live such long lives, and the records show that after the flood, within just several generations, people were living much shorter lives than before the flood."

Because they were faithful and trusted God, God changed Abram's name to Abraham, and Sarai's name to Sarah. Abraham and Sarah loved their little boy, Isaac. He was growing up into a beautiful young man, and then something happened that shook Abraham to the core.

God spoke clearly to Abraham, "Abraham!"

"Here I am," he replied.

"Take your son—your only son, Isaac—whom you love, and go to the region of Moriah. Sacrifice him there as a burnt offering on one of the mountains I will tell you about."

Abraham was in shock. God had asked him to do this awful thing even after he and Sarah had obeyed God and had waited all this time for this promised son. Now God was asking him to kill his son as a sacrifice for his sins. But God's command was clear, and Abraham obeyed.

It is important that we take note here that Abraham is a very special person in the Bible. He obeyed God even when he was being asked to do something that was really, really hard and almost impossible to do. He just obeyed when God spoke to him, even when it didn't make sense.

So Abraham took Isaac to the place where God led him, and they built an altar together. After the altar was prepared, Abraham tied up his son and laid him on the altar. Then he reached out his hand and took the knife to slay his son. But just then, the angel of the Lord called out to him from heaven. "Abraham! Abraham!"

"Here I am," he replied.

"Do not lay a hand on the boy," the angel said. "Do not do anything to him. Now I know that you fear God, because you have not withheld from me your son, your only son."

Abraham looked up, and there in a thicket was a ram, caught by his horns. He went over and took the ram and sacrificed it as a burnt offering instead of his son.

The Lord said to Abraham, "because you have done this and have not withheld your only son, I will surely bless you and make your descendants as numerous as the stars in the sky. Your descendants will take possession of the cities of their enemies, and through your offspring, all the nations on earth will be blessed, because you have obeyed me."

"Anna, why did God ask Abraham to do this terrible thing?" Papa asked.

"God was testing him to see if he would obey."

Papa nodded. "That's right. God knew that if Abraham would obey that terrible command, then he would do anything that God asked of him. This is a really important story to remember, Anna and Lily. One day, many years later, God would send His own Son down to earth knowing that His own Son would become a sin offering for all those who would believe in Him. Not only was God testing Abraham, but He was showing all of us just how serious He is about sin, and He wanted to teach us that all sins must be punished. Lily, can you think of a harder test for Abraham?"

"No."

"God knew that Abraham was indeed worthy to be the Father of the Special Nation. This Nation would be a key in God's plan to make it possible for people to get back to the garden."

So Isaac grew into a young man and married a beautiful girl named Rebecca. When Isaac was forty years old, Rebecca became pregnant with twins.

Lily jumped down off Papa's lap and said, "Papa, it's hard for me to understand all this stuff. Why is the Bible so hard to understand?"

Papa smiled at his beautiful little granddaughter and replied, "You are absolutely right, Lily. This long story about God's plan can get really confusing and tiring. If it's hard for an old man like me, I can imagine that it's really hard for a little girl like you."

Let's review what we've learned so far:

1. God created everything: the earth, the stars, the animals, and man.
2. People were made special. God wanted to love the people and walk with them in the garden forever.
3. God gave man free will, which meant that man could make choices. He could even choose to disobey God.
4. When man disobeys, he is separated from God.
5. Even before God created the world, God knew that men would disobey.
6. Satan is real, and he is always trying hard to get man to turn away from God.
7. God had a plan for man to be made right with God once again. We call this God's plan of salvation.
8. This plan would take several thousand years to be completed.
9. God's plan of salvation is what the Old Testament is all about.

Study Guide for Chapter 7 – Obeying God's Promise

Story 7: Obeying God's Promise
Read: Genesis 11:26, Genesis 12:1–3, Genesis 22:1–2, Genesis 22:15–18
Read: Papa's Story 7

Papa's Comments

After the flood, the three sons of Noah all start having families, and this new world begins to be populated all over again. The Word of God was passed down from Adam to his son Seth, and then eventually to Noah and then to his son Shem. Just like before the flood, there was a line of believers, but the great majority of men rejected the truth. The Word of God was being passed down through this thin line of believers.

Review Genesis 11:26 (Abraham is in the line of Shem).

A man named Abram was one of Shem's great-great-great (twelve *great*s) descendants. Abram was in this special line of men who believed in God and in God's Word.

Review Genesis 12:1–3 (God's promise to Abraham).

The promise that God makes to this seventy-five-year-old man, Abram, is the beginning of a very long story. This promise includes several significant components, and it also has a very important condition that Abraham has to satisfy. Understanding this promise is a key to understanding what the Old Testament is all about.

The Promise:

1. Abraham's family would become a great nation.
2. This nation would be given a special land.
3. Abraham and his family would be greatly blessed.
4. All the families on the earth would be blessed through Abraham and his family.

The Condition

1. Abraham had to obey God and get up, leave his home, and go off to a strange land. Abraham was being asked to trust God. Leaving the security of his home and going off to an unknown and hostile land took a great deal of faith in God.

Discussion and Questions:

Think about the title that Papa gave this chapter, "Obeying God's Promise." We don't usually think of promises as something that we must obey. However, the promise that God makes to Abraham also has a requirement that Abraham must meet in order to receive the rewards of the promise. God wants Abraham to be totally obedient, to trust and obey God, even when what God is asking doesn't seem to make any sense.

1. Review Genesis 12:1–3. What does God ask Abraham to do? Would this be easy or hard? Do you think Abraham had to trust God in order to do what God asked? What does Abraham do?
2. Review Genesis 22:1–2. What does God ask Abraham to do? Would this be easy or hard? Do you think Abraham had to trust God in order to do what God asked? What does Abraham do?
3. Review Genesis 22:15–18. Because Abraham obeyed God (even when it didn't make any sense), God repeats the original promise that He had made to Abraham so many years before. Remember how patient Noah had to be and how long he had to keep on trusting God before the flood came? Did that patience pay off for Noah in the end? Now Abraham's patience is going to be rewarded. The remainder of the Old Testament is all about God keeping every aspect to the promise to Abraham.

Summary of Chapter 7: Understanding the Old Testament

This promise to Abraham is a big key to understanding the Old Testament. The Word of God now included the promise to Abraham. The Word would be passed down from one generation to the next through a thin line of believers (men of faith). The Old Testament is a long, long story of God delivering on His part of the promise. This long, long story is all about God's plan for men to find their way back to the garden.

One final thought: Sacrificing your only son is about as hard as it gets. Does this story of Abraham and Isaac remind you of another story of a son being sacrificed?

Chapter 8

The Tribe of Israel

Anna and Lily Loving Life

Genesis 27–50
Jacob Has Twelve Sons
Joseph's Brothers Sell Him as a Slave
Joseph Becomes a Powerful Man in Egypt
Jacob (Israel) and Entire Family Move to Egypt

The Promised Land

Sally had to attend a school meeting. She called Papa to see if he could stop over for a few hours and watch the girls. When Papa arrived, the girls were in the playroom making a loud ruckus with their Wii guitars. Papa got settled on the couch and turned on the evening news. The president was just about to start another speech on the economy when the girls came bursting into the room.

"Papa, good, you're here!" exclaimed Lily. "Where's Grammy?"

"Grammy doesn't feel real good, so I'm the big man in charge," Papa answered.

"Can you tell us the next story, Papa?" Anna asked.

"I'm glad you asked, since I was planning on it, and I really didn't want to watch the news and listen to Mr. Obama make another long-winded speech." Papa smiled. "Let's get comfortable, and after the story, I have a big surprise for you—that is, if you promise that when it's time, you'll both go to bed without a fight."

"Okay, Papa. We promise." Anna sighed.

"Now let's get to today's story. In last week's story, God promised that Abraham would be the father of a great nation. Abraham needed lots of children and grandchildren, and he and Sarah were clearly too old to have any more children. Abraham's son Isaac was the only way that this could happen. Isaac married a beautiful girl named Rebecka. Rebecka became pregnant with twins, and they named them Esau and Jacob."

Papa looked at his two granddaughters and continued, "Many of these Bible stories get real long and complicated. If I told you the whole story of Esau and Jacob, I'm pretty sure that you would get pretty bored, so I'll just tell you the short version. Someday when you're older, you should read the whole story. There are some pretty interesting things to learn."

The Short Story of Esau and Jacob

"If we think all the way back to Adam and his sons, we will remember that God's Word passed down from Adam to Seth, and then one of Seth's sons, Enosh, accepted God's Word, and he in turn passed it on down to one of his sons—and on and on. Then after the flood, Noah passed the Word on down to Shem, and this continued all the way to Abraham, and then his son Isaac and then his son Jacob.

"If we lined up all these believers, we would have twenty-two men lined up from Adam to Jacob. In other words, Adam is Jacob's great-great-great-great-great-great-great-great-great-great, plus fourteen more *greats*, grandfather. And God's special blessing and Word to Adam passed down through this special line of men."

Papa stopped for a second. "I said that Rebekah and Isaac had twins and only one of them received this blessing from Isaac. The problem was, Esau was the older twin, and traditionally, he was to receive the blessing. But God had different plans. God knew Jacob's heart and character, and it was God's plan to have His Word and the blessing pass on to Jacob, not Esau.

"Jacob tricked Isaac into giving him the blessing. I'm not going to go into the long story of this trick of Jacob's, but I will tell you that Esau was very angry at Jacob, and Jacob had to run away for a long time in order to be safe from Esau. Jacob escaped to his grandfather Abraham's hometown of Ur. He was safe there, and he found a wife—several wives, in fact. Jacob began having children, and the nation that God promised to Abraham was beginning to grow. Eventually Jacob had twelve sons, and one day, God told him to return to the promised land, the land that God had promised to Abraham."

Papa looked at his little granddaughters. "Are you able to follow this story okay? Or is this too complicated?"

"It's hard to follow, but I think I get it," replied Lily.

Anna said, "I can follow the story okay, but I don't always understand why God does things the way He does them."

"I'm with you, Anna. Sometimes I don't understand why God does things the way He does. But the older I get and the more I study God's Word, the more it all makes sense. When I was a kid, I often didn't understand my parents and why they wouldn't let me do some things. As I got older, and then became a parent myself, I started to understand their point of view better and better. It's like that with God and His plan—the more you study it, the more it makes sense.

"Let's get back to the story. So Jacob obeys God, just like Abraham, and goes back to the land that was promised to Abraham. But he and his family are still foreigners, and many of the people who live there are hostile to them. Because they don't really own any land, they have to live in tents, and they have to move from time to time. The years went by, and Jacob's family kept growing as his sons and their wives had children of their own. Later, we will see that the families of these twelve sons would eventually become the twelve tribes of Israel."

Papa continued, "Because Jacob trusted God and did what God asked him to do, God gave Jacob a new name. He named him Israel. Jacob's family became known as the Tribe of Israel. Jacob's eleventh son was named Joseph, and he was Jacob's favorite son. Because Jacob loved Joseph so much, Joseph's older brothers became very jealous. Israel's ten older boys would often have to leave the camp to take the herds where there was good grass to eat, but Jacob would keep Joseph home with him. Then something happened that made the older sons absolutely furious with Joseph—so furious that they wanted to kill him."

"What happened, Papa?" Anna asked.

"Joseph had a dream, and he told it to his brothers. He said to them, 'Listen to this dream I had: We were binding sheaves of grain out in the field when suddenly my sheaf stood straight up, while your sheaves gathered around mine and bowed down to it.' His brothers said to him, 'Do you intend to rule over us?' Then Joseph told his brothers and his father another dream: 'In my dream, the sun and the moon and eleven stars were all bowing down to me.'"

Even Israel scolded his favorite son, and said, "What is this dream you had? Will your mother and I and your eleven brothers actually come before you and bow down?"

Now, more than ever, the brothers really hated their arrogant little brother.

Not long after that, Joseph's older brothers were away from the camp tending the flocks of sheep. Israel asked Joseph if he would go and see how they were doing and then report back. When the brothers saw Joseph coming, they plotted to kill him, but one of the brothers argued against that. So they decided to sell him as a slave to a group of people who were travelling to Egypt. They were sure that there was no chance that they would ever have to see their hated brother ever again.

But it turns out that this was all a part of God's big plan.

"What happened next, Papa?" asked Lily.

"Joseph gets carried off to Egypt as a slave, and his brothers go home to Jacob, and they tell Jacob that Joseph must have been eaten by a lion. They had covered Joseph's coat with the blood of an animal, and they told their father that it was Joseph's blood. Israel was miserable. His favorite son was dead.

"Here's where the story gets interesting: Joseph becomes a slave in the home of a wealthy man who has a wife. The wife loved Joseph because he was very handsome and charming. One day, when her husband was away, she tried to get Joseph to come close to her, but Joseph refused her, because Joseph knew that God would disapprove. Joseph, it turns out, was a lot like Abraham. He had faith in God and had committed his life to obeying Him. The lady was furious with Joseph, and when her husband returned home, she lied to him, saying that Joseph had tried to get close to her. So her husband had Joseph put in a prison."

Papa took a breath and continued, "This is a long story, and somewhat complicated, but try hard to follow it. As we get to the end of the story, we'll be able to see that all of this is a part of God's plan."

So Joseph is in prison. It turns out that at the same time, Pharaoh, the king of Egypt, got angry with two of his servants, his cupbearer and his baker, and he had the two of them thrown into the same prison as Joseph. Then something happened: each of those men had dreams on the same night, and each dream had a meaning of its own. They both were upset because no one was able to interpret the dreams. When Joseph saw the two men, he asked them why they were upset, and they told him why.

Joseph said to them, "Interpretations belong to God. Tell me your dreams."

So the cupbearer told Joseph his dream. He said, "In my dream I saw a vine in front of me, and on the vine were three branches. As soon as it budded, it blossomed, and its clusters ripened into grapes. Pharaoh's cup was in my hand, and I took the grapes, squeezed them into Pharaoh's cup, and put the cup into his hand."

Joseph said to the cupbearer, "The three branches are three days. Within three days, Pharaoh will restore you to your position and you will put Pharaoh's cup into his hand, just as you used to. Now please remember me when you're free from prison, for I am in prison and I have done nothing wrong."

Clearly, God had told Joseph the meaning of the cupbearer's dream.

Then the baker told Joseph his dream. "There were three baskets of bread on my head. In the top basket were all kinds of baked goods for Pharaoh, but the birds were eating them out of the basket on my head."

Joseph said to the baker, "The three baskets are three days. Within three days, Pharaoh will cut off your head and hang you on a tree, and the birds will eat away your flesh."

"So what happened, Papa?" asked Anna.

"In three days, the cupbearer was brought back to Pharaoh's palace and given back his old job. The baker's head was cut off, and he was hung on a tree, where the birds ate his flesh. Everything happened exactly as Joseph said it would. God had told Joseph how to interpret the dreams."

Several years went by, and Joseph was still in prison. The cupbearer had forgotten his promise to Joseph to tell Pharaoh about letting Joseph out of prison. But then something happened. The king, the Pharaoh, had a dream. He was really bothered by this dream, and he asked all his wise men to interpret his dream for him, but none of them could.

Then Pharaoh had a second dream, and once again, none of his wise men could understand the dream or interpret it for him. The dreams were so clear in Pharaoh's mind, and he was really bothered by them. Then Pharaoh's cupbearer remembered Joseph and the way that Joseph had correctly interpreted his dream and the dream of the baker. The cupbearer told Pharaoh, and immediately Pharaoh sent for Joseph.

When Joseph stood before Pharaoh, Pharaoh said, "I had a dream, and no one can interpret it. I have heard that you are able to interpret dreams."

Joseph replied, "I cannot do it, but God can."

So Pharaoh told Joseph his dreams, and when he was finished, Joseph said, "The two dreams are the same. God has revealed to Pharaoh what he is about to do. Seven years of great abundance are coming throughout the land of Egypt, but seven years of great famine will follow them. Then all the abundance in Egypt will be forgotten, and famine will ravage the land. The good years will not be remembered because the famine will be so severe. God has decided that this will happen soon. Pharaoh should look for a wise man and put him in charge of the land of Egypt. Let Pharaoh appoint commissioners over the land to take a fifth of the harvest of Egypt during the good years. They should store up grain during these years so that there is enough saved for the bad years."

Then Pharaoh said, "Since God has made all of this known to you, Joseph, there is no one in Egypt wiser than you. I, Pharaoh, put you, Joseph, in charge of the whole land of Egypt."

Then Pharaoh put his ring on Joseph's finger.

Papa looked at his two little granddaughters. "So what do you think of that? Joseph gets sold into slavery by his own brothers, and several years later, he's the number two most powerful person in the land of Egypt, the most powerful nation in the world."

"What happened then, Papa?" asked Anna.

"The land of Egypt had seven great years, and all that time, Joseph was busy storing up the grain, saving it up for the seven bad years. Then just as God had told Joseph through Pharaoh's dreams, a great famine began all over the land, not only in Egypt but also all over the world. Jacob, Joseph's father, and his sons and their families suffered from the famine also. There was no food anywhere except in Egypt."

Finally, Jacob and his eleven sons were desperate. They were starving. Jacob told his sons to travel to Egypt, where they had heard that there were stores filled with food. Jacob gave them gold to purchase the grain.

When they arrived, Joseph recognized his brothers, but they didn't recognize him. They never imagined they would ever see him again. But even after all that had been done to Joseph, he still loved his brothers. Remember, Joseph was a believer in God, and God's spirit lived in him. He could forgive his brothers, even though they had sold him into slavery. Also, Joseph knew that God could use the evil thing that they had done to him for His own plan. All these amazing things that had happened to Joseph—the slavery, the dreams, the powerful position— were part of God's plan for the nation of Israel to become a blessing to the whole world.

Joseph knows that the famine will continue for several more years and that Jacob's family will not survive if they stay in Canaan. Somehow, Joseph was able to forgive the terrible wrong that his brothers had done to him. So he makes a plan to get the whole family, including Jacob, to Egypt, where Joseph can protect them during these really difficult times. Remember, Joseph is rich and powerful now and has all kinds of influence and power.

The brothers still do not know that Joseph is their brother. Joseph's plan involves taking one brother captive and then forcing the other brothers to go back to Canaan and gather the entire family and return to Egypt in order for them to free their brother. They still don't know that Joseph is their brother. They return to Canaan and tell Jacob that the entire family has to go to Egypt in order to get their brother back. The famine rages on. There is really no choice, so Jacob and the entire tribe, including the wives and children, go to Egypt.

When they arrive, Joseph reveals himself, and there is a happy reunion. Jacob has his beloved son Joseph back. The brothers, who have been forgiven, realize that Joseph has forgiven them and still loves them. Joseph gives them a nice area in Egypt to build homes, and the Tribe of Israel settles down in Egypt.

Study Guide for Chapter 8 – The Tribe of Israel

Story 8: The Tribe of Israel
Read: Papa's Story 8

Summarize the story of the sons of Isaac, Esau, and Jacob: Jacob tricks Esau out of the inheritance of Isaac, and thus, Jacob becomes the son who will continue carrying forth the promise that was made to his grandfather, Abraham.

Recall the Promise: God had promised Abraham that if he would trust God completely, then God would make the descendants of Abraham a great nation, and that this great nation would eventually live in a beautiful Promised Land of their own.

The remainder of the book of Genesis (from Genesis 27–50) is the long story of Abraham's and Jacob's descendants becoming a great nation.

The book of Exodus is the story of this great nation taking possession of a beautiful Promised Land.

What was the third part of the promise made to Abraham?

Discussion Questions

1. When Joseph stood before Pharaoh and was asked to interpret Pharaoh's dreams, what did Joseph say? Did Joseph trust God?
2. We know that God told Abraham to leave his country and go to a faraway land. The Bible doesn't tell us how God spoke to Abraham. Somehow, Abraham knew it was God telling him to go. What are some ways that God could have spoken to Abraham? How do you think God spoke to Joseph?

3. How does God speak to us today? Has He ever spoken to you? How did He speak to you, and how do you know it was Him speaking?
4. Selling Joseph as a slave was an evil act on the part of Joseph's brothers. However, this evil act was a part of God's

plan. God was in the process of keeping His promise to Abraham. This special family of Jacob (the grandson of Abraham) was to become the large nation of Israel, and having Joseph become a Prince of Egypt was all a part of this plan. Does God know the future?
5. Can God use the evil acts of men for His own good purposes?
6. Is Brewster's a great place for ice cream?

Chapter 9

Israel, Moses, and Miracles

Moses Stands before Pharaoh

Exodus 3–14
For 450 Years, and the Israelites Are Slaves in Egypt
The Tribe of Israel Grows to a Nation of Millions
Moses Asks Pharaoh, "Let My People Go"
The Exodus Begins

PAPA'S STORIES

"We'd love to watch the kids, honey," Grammy replied to Sally's request. "You and Sean deserve a special night out together. We'll be there by five-thirty." She put down the phone and went to the bottom of the stairs, where she called up to Papa, "Brian, after your shower, we're going over to babysit Anna and Lily for a couple of hours. Try to hurry, because I promised that we'd be there in fifteen minutes."

Sally and Maddie—the Conroys' beagle—met Grammy and Papa at the door.

"Thanks for doing this at the last second," Sally said. "Sean and I really need a break. We should be back by eight. Dinner's in the oven."

Thirty minutes later, Grammy, Papa, and the kids were finishing up the tuna casserole that Sally had prepared.

Lily asked, "Can you tell us the next story, Papa?"

"I was hoping that one of you would ask," Papa responded. "It's called 'Israel, Moses, and Miracles.' Everybody, put your plates in the dishwasher, and let's get comfortable on the couch."

Two minutes later, Papa began. "The last story was mostly about one of Jacob's sons, Joseph. Do you remember what happened to Joseph?"

"His brothers sold him as a slave, and then they told their father that he had been killed," Anna replied.

Lily added, "And he went to Egypt and was put in jail. Then he got out of jail because people were having crazy dreams and Joseph could tell what those dreams meant."

"Very good! How did last week's story end?"

Anna said, "The king put Joseph in charge of the land, and he had the people save up tons of food because the king's dreams told him that there would be a famine. Then there was a famine, and people from all over the world had to go to Egypt to get food. Joseph's brothers came for food, and Joseph saw them. Then he tricked them into bringing the whole family to Egypt. Finally, Joseph told them who he was."

"Was Joseph still angry with his brothers for selling him as a slave?" Papa asked.

"No," replied Lily. "He had forgiven them."

We learn from that story that God can use the evil deeds of men for His good purpose. What the brothers did was evil, but in the end, having Joseph in Egypt turned out to save the Tribe of Israel from starvation. I think we're ready for this week's story.

So Joseph has his father, his mother, and all eleven brothers in Egypt. They brought all their wives and children. The Tribe of Israel was probably made up of about one hundred total people at that time. Joseph gave them an area outside of the city where they could build homes and live. They did not mix with the Egyptians and kept to themselves, but they were safe.

"What does this story have to do with the Bible, Papa?" Anna asked. "What's the big deal about this particular family?"

"Remember that God had a plan to help men find a way back to the garden. One key part of that plan was a promise made to Abraham. A great nation would come from Abraham. This family living in Egypt is the beginning of that nation of promise. Keeping this family alive and together was critical to the plan. What were the other parts of that promise to Abraham?"

Lily raised her hand. "I know, Papa. This nation would live in the Promised Land. That land wasn't in Egypt, was it?"

"Good answer, Lily. The Promised Land was not in Egypt, so this part of the promise still had to happen in the future. Was there anything else to the promise?"

"The whole world would be blessed," answered Anna.

"Good answer, Anna. Over the course of these stories, we'll see that that this plan of God is what the Bible is all about. Over four hundred years go by, and the Tribe of Israel is still living in this same area of Egypt. Of course Joseph, and Jacob, and his brothers and their families have all died off. But their great-great-great…grandchildren are all still living there. We have to stop here and look closely at this remarkable family.

"First, they have multiplied many times in numbers. Amazingly, they now number over two million men, women, and children. Second, they have stayed together as a family and have not mixed in with the population of Egypt. If they had mixed in with the

Egyptians, they would no longer be a distinct family. Last, the Word of God and the promise to Abraham was passed down from generation to generation. As always, there were some true believers, and there were many who did not believe. The Tribe of Israel is now the large nation of Israel."

"Why was this nation still in Egypt? Why didn't they just go to the Promised Land?" asked Anna.

"Finally, Pharaoh died and then Joseph died. The new king of Egypt decided to make the Israelites into slaves. He forced them to stay separate from the Egyptians, but he wouldn't let them leave Egypt because they were getting all kinds of free labor out of them. The Egyptians hated and feared the Israelites, and the Israelites hated their cruel masters, the Egyptians."

"So what happened next, Papa?" asked Lily.

"Over four hundred years go by, and the Israelites are still enslaved by the hated Egyptians. Then the evil king of Egypt decided that the Israelites had grown too large, and he ordered that all the Jewish baby boys had to be killed. A young Israelite mother had a baby boy and tried to save him by placing him in a basket and she sent him down the Nile River. He was rescued by the women who lived in the king's palace, and they allowed him to live and to grow up in the palace. Many years later, this young man named Moses had to escape from Egypt because he had killed an Egyptian who was especially cruel to the Israelites. For years, Moses lived out in the wilderness, and then one day, God spoke clearly to Moses. He told Moses to go back to Egypt and to stand before the king and ask him to let the people of Israel leave."

"Why would Pharaoh let the people go?" asked Lily.

"God told Moses that He would give Moses special miraculous powers when he stood before Pharaoh, so that Pharaoh would have to pay attention to him."

Anna asked, "What do you mean by special miraculous powers?"

"God told Moses that in order to show Pharaoh that Moses was speaking on the authority of the One True God, Moses would be able to threaten the Nation of Egypt with some terrible plagues if Pharaoh didn't let the people of Israel go free."

"What are terrible plagues, Papa?" Lily questioned. "I don't know that word."

"Plagues are terrible things that happen to a large group of people. Let me continue, and I think you'll understand. Moses went before Pharaoh and told him that the God of Israel wanted Pharaoh to let the Israelites go free. Pharaoh told Moses that he didn't have any respect for the God of Israel.

"Show me a miracle." Pharaoh laughed at Moses. "So I may believe in this God of yours."

Moses did what God had told him to do. He threw his staff down on the ground in front of Pharaoh. Immediately God turned the staff into a large snake. But Pharaoh had some clever magicians who threw down their staffs, and by their sorcery, their staffs also turned into snakes. But the snake of Moses swallowed up the snakes of Pharaoh's magicians. This was to show that the God of the Israelites was the One True God and was all-powerful. But Pharaoh had a hard heart and refused Moses's request.

The next day, Moses went back before Pharaoh and told him that the God of Israel would turn all the water in Egypt into blood, and that is exactly what happened. All the water turned to blood, the fish in the rivers all died, and the people had nothing to drink. But Pharaoh still refused to let the people go.

Seven days later, Moses went back and told Pharaoh that the God of Israel would cause frogs to cover the land of Egypt. Moses waved his staff out over the rivers and canals, and millions of frogs came up out of the water and covered the land. The frogs went into everybody's home, and finally, Pharaoh agreed to let the people go. So Moses prayed and God stopped the plague of frogs. But when Pharaoh saw that the plague was over, he went back on his word and again refused to let the people go.

Nine times God sent terrible plagues, and every time, Pharaoh refused.

"What were some of the other plagues?" asked Anna.

"One was that all the dust in Egypt would turn into little gnats. Then God sent a plague of flies, and swarms of flies filled every house in Egypt. However, there were no flies in Goshen where the Israelites lived. Then God caused all the men of Egypt and animals to be covered with festering boils. Then God had all the cattle belonging to the Egyptians die, but none of the cattle of the Israelites died.

"Still Pharaoh refused. The Bible says that Pharaoh's heart had become hardened. Then God caused it to hail on Egypt, and every man or animal caught in the storm died. It did not hail in Goshen. Then God sent the plague of locusts. These little grasshoppers completely covered the land of Egypt so that the ground could not be seen. They devoured everything growing in the fields. Still Pharaoh refused to let the Israelites go."

Papa looked at his two little granddaughters. "Can you believe that Pharaoh still refused? By now, wouldn't you think he would believe that this God of Moses was all-powerful? Let me tell you something: God had hardened Pharaoh's heart because He wanted to show all the people His awesome power. Moses clearly gave all the credit to God for all these amazing things, and all the people knew that the God of Abraham, Isaac, and Jacob was the One True and All-Powerful God. Because Pharaoh kept refusing to let the people go, God could keep on showing these incredible miracles. Because this was happening in Egypt, which was the most powerful nation on earth, the whole world would soon hear about this awesome God of Israel. This was all a part of God's plan. There were still two more plagues to go before this story is over.

"The next plague was three days of total darkness in Egypt. No Egyptian could see each other or leave their home for three full days. And yet the Israelites had light where they lived nearby."

Papa continued, "The last plague was by far the worst. To show all the people His awesome power, He had Moses tell each Israelite family to make a sin offering of a lamb. He told them to paint their doorposts with the blood of the lamb and they would be safe from the plague. They were also instructed to get ready to leave Egypt the next day, that this plague would be the one that would convince Pharaoh that even he should obey God's demands."

"What was this terrible plague, Papa?" asked Lily.

"God told Moses that His Spirit would kill the firstborn son of every family that did not sacrifice a lamb and follow His instructions.

The Israelites obeyed, and God's Spirit 'passed over' their homes. The Egyptians did not obey God. The next day, a great cry went up in Egypt. The firstborn son of every family never woke up. They were all dead, even Pharaoh's son. Now Pharaoh was finally convinced that he had to let the Israelites leave.

"Just imagine what the next day was like. Over two million people with all their belongings began a slow march out of Egypt. The great Exodus had begun, and the second part of God's promise to Abraham was beginning to come to pass. God had indeed made Israel into a great nation, and now He was leading His special people to the land He had promised Abraham so many years before. There's still a lot more to this story of the Exodus from Egypt, but now, it's time for all of us to have a bowl of ice cream, and we'll continue this story next week."

Study Guide for Chapter 9 – Israel, Moses and Miracles

Story 9: Israel, Moses, and Miracles
Read: Exodus 3–14
Read: Papa's Story 9

In the previous chapter, Joseph's brothers had sold Joseph as a slave into Egypt. This evil act was used by God to save the small tribe of Israel from starvation. Now the whole family was relocated from Canaan and into Egypt. They had been saved from starvation, but before long, Pharaoh died, and the next king decided to make slaves of these foreigners. The Israelites were isolated into a special area named Goshen, and they were forced to work really hard for the Egyptians.

What had happened to God's promise to Abraham? This slavery and isolation was all a part of God's plan. Because they were slaves and isolated, they could not mix in with the Egyptian population. If they had mixed in with the Egyptians, over time, this special family of Israel would simply blend into the general population, and it would cease to exist as a special and distinct family. However, because they were isolated and not allowed to mix, this family stayed together, and after over 450 years, it had grown to over two million people. The Tribe of Israel was now the very large and well-defined Nation of Israel. The promise of becoming a large nation that God had made to Abraham had been kept. But the promises of this nation having its own special land and the promise of being a blessing to the whole world still had not been fulfilled. Papa's Story 9 tells of how God continued to complete the promise that He had made to Abraham so many years before.

Discussion Questions

1. In the previous story, Joseph's brothers sold Joseph into slavery. God turned this evil act into a great blessing for the family of Israel. Then an evil Pharaoh took advantage

of this family and forced the entire tribe into slavery. Once again, God used an evil act for His own purposes. This isolated family would grow into a large nation of people, and a major part of God's promise to Abraham would be fulfilled. What were some of the other promises that God still had to keep?

2. Egypt was the most powerful and important nation on earth during this time. When Pharaoh kept refusing Moses's request to let the Israelites leave Egypt, the whole world was watching. Plague after terrible plague, and Pharaoh kept refusing to let the people leave. Doesn't it seem unreasonable that Pharaoh would keep on refusing Moses's request? The Bible says that God hardened Pharaoh's heart. Why would God do that?

Concluding Thoughts

During the last plague, the Israelites were told to sacrifice a lamb and paint the blood over their doorposts. By doing this, they could save their families from this last plague. This was to be remembered by the Israelites and celebrated with the Feast of the Passover. Today, Christians see this as a symbol of how the blood of the Lamb of God is a major key to their salvation. Remember, the Old Testament is the story of how God's people can return to the garden.

Chapter 10

The Exodus and the Wilderness

The Ten Commandments

Exodus 14–20 and Numbers 13–16
The Exodus
The Parting of the Red Sea
Manna from Heaven and Water from a Rock
The Twelve Spies
Forty Years of Trusting God

"Hi, girls."

"Hi, Papa. Are you going to tell us the next story?" Anna asked.

"I'm ready if you are. This story is really a continuation of last week's story. After the ten plagues, the king of Egypt finally let the Israelites leave. Moses would lead them to the long-ago Promised Land.

"This large group of over two million people had left Egypt, but they really didn't know how they were going to be able to live in the land that God had promised them. The land between Egypt and the Promised Land was all mountains and desert. It was called the wilderness, and it was virtually uninhabitable. They just had to follow Moses and God, and have lots of faith. God made a large pillar of a cloud to appear in front of this large group, and this strange cloud led the people during the day. At night, the pillar would change to a pillar of fire, and it would light the way for the people to follow. Clearly, God was in charge of this Exodus.

"The people followed the pillar, and eventually, they came up on the Red Sea. There was no way to cross. When they looked back behind them, they were terrified to see that Pharaoh had sent out his powerful army with hundreds of chariots. Pharaoh had broken his promise again and was going to force the people back to Egypt. The people were stuck—the sea was in front and Pharaoh's army was in back.

"Then once again, God made an amazing miracle happen. God told Moses to hold out his rod over the sea. Right in front of this large group of frightened people, the waters of the sea began to part. The floor of the sea became like a dry roadway to the other side. With great fear, the people stepped forward onto this miraculous path, and inside steep walls of water, they began the long walk across. In the meantime, Pharaoh's army was held back by the large pillar of fire.

"Finally, all the Israelites had made it safely across the sea. Then God's pillar of fire allowed Pharaoh's army to chase after the Israelites, and when they were all in the middle of the sea, God caused the walls of water to collapse, and the entire Egyptian army was drowned. This was an amazing miracle, and over two million Israelites had lived through it. Surely, now they would all totally trust in this most impressive God, the God of Abraham, Isaac, Jacob, Moses—and now the God of the Nation of Israel. Their God could deliver them from anything. They just had to trust and obey."

"What happened to all these people now, Papa?" asked Lily. "What was it like on the other side of the sea?"

"I'm glad you asked, Lily. A whole bunch of interesting things happened. God still had many things to teach the people, and this was the perfect time and place to teach. The people were now free from Egypt and safe from Pharaoh's army, but there wasn't anything to eat. They went to Moses and began to complain loudly. Then God did something amazing: He caused bread to rain down from the sky. This bread was the perfect food and satisfied their hunger and provided them with all the necessary vitamins and minerals that they needed to live. It rained down bread. Imagine that. All the people had to do was to go out and gather it.

"Some of the people thought that they would gather a whole bunch more than they needed and then they wouldn't need to go out and gather the following day. But when they looked at the bread they had stored up the next day, it was all covered with ugly bugs, and they had to throw it out. Can either of you girls figure out what God was teaching them? This is something that we should remember too."

"I'm not sure," Lily answered. "Do you know, Anna?"

Anna answered, "I think that God wanted the people to learn to trust Him on a day-by-day basis. They had to learn to ask Him for their daily bread, to ask for just what they needed that day and not any more than that."

"What a great answer, Anna."

Papa continued the story. "The Israelites were running out of water, and there was no fresh water anywhere around. God told Moses to touch a large rock with his staff, and a river of water began flowing from the rock. So now the people were eating bread from heaven and drinking water flowing from a rock. God was surely taking care of this special group of people. You would think that they could trust God to do anything.

"The Israelites camped out at the base of a large mountain, Mt. Sinai. God covered the mountain in smoke and told Moses to go up the mountain alone. When Moses returned several days later, he had two large stone tablets that God had engraved with the Ten Commandments. Do you all know the Ten Commandments?"

"Love the Lord your God. That was the first one, I think," answered Lily.

"Obey your parents," offered Anna.

"Don't work on Sundays," added Lily. "Don't use bad language."

"Don't kill anybody," said Anna.

"That's five. Good job," Papa said approvingly. "Can we get any more?"

Papa continued, "Be faithful to your spouse. And do not steal from others."

Lily jumped in with, "'Don't tell lies' is one, and 'Don't worship idols' is another."

Anna added, "I think another one is that we should not covet what other people have."

"What does that one mean?" Lily asked. "I don't know the word *covet*."

"*Covet* means 'to be jealous,'" Papa said. "The verse means that we should be happy with what we have and we should not always be wishing that we had stuff that other people have.

"Good job, everybody!" Papa exclaimed. "I think you got all ten. Now that we know them, we should start obeying them. Can any of you think of a time when you've broken one of these commandments? I certainly can. As a matter of fact, I've broken all of them."

"You have not, Papa." Anna laughed. "You never killed anyone."

"You're right, Anna, *and* you're wrong," Papa said. "You're right that I have never killed anyone's body, but you're also wrong. There have been some people who I disliked so much I actually found myself wishing they were dead. In a very real way, in my heart, I broke God's commandment. I'm afraid that I've broken all of the commandments. I've certainly told lies, and I've used language that was not honoring to God. I've done plenty of coveting, and I have lots of idols that prevent me from worshiping God the way I should. I'd go on, but you wouldn't think very well of me if I did.

"God told Moses to move the people onward to the Promised Land and He would deliver it to them. So the Israelites broke camp, and after several days, they found themselves on the border of the land that God had promised Abraham so many years before. But they faced a big problem: this land already had hundreds of cities and thousands of people living there. Certainly these people would not allow two million strangers to come walking in and start living there.

"So the Israelites set up camp and decided to send in twelve spies to check out the land and to help them decide how to proceed. Several weeks later, the spies returned and made their report to Moses and the leaders. Do either of you know what they reported?"

"I don't," Lily responded. "Do you, Anna?"

"Me neither." Anna shook her head.

"All twelve of the spies agreed that the land was beautiful, and, the way they said it, 'It flows with milk and honey.' Two of the spies, Caleb and Joshua, said, 'We should go up now and take the land and with our God leading us and protecting us, we can do it.'

"But ten of the spies still didn't have faith. 'We can't attack those people,' they said. 'They are stronger than we are. There are giants living there, and we are like grasshoppers to them.'

"There was a big argument among the leaders of the people. Moses, along with Joshua and Caleb, argued strongly that God would protect his special nation—but only if they would trust and obey Him. Moses argued that God wanted them to go into the land and He would deliver it to them. The other ten spies argued that the people had big walls around their cities, they were trained to fight wars, and that the Nation of Israel would have no chance of winning against such an enemy."

Anna interrupted, "How could the people forget all the things that God had done for them so soon?"

"I asked that same question, Anna, the first time I read that story," Papa replied. "Just think, these same people had just witnessed the ten great plagues of Egypt—all miracles—and then the parting of the Red Sea and the destruction of the powerful Egyptian army, an amazing miracle. In addition to all of that, they were living on bread falling down from heaven and water from a rock. These were daily reminders that the God of Israel could be trusted totally. All they had to do was trust and obey."

Papa continued, "Moses, Joshua, and Caleb eventually lost the argument, and the people refused to go into the land. God, of course, knew that this would happen. He knew their hearts, and He knew that when the time of decision came the big majority of these people would not have faith in Him, even after all that God had done. With the exception of Moses, Joshua, Caleb, and a few others, these were not the people that He wanted to deliver into the land that He had promised Abraham."

"So what happened, Papa?" asked Lily. "The people couldn't really go back to Egypt. How would they live? They couldn't keep living out in the desert, could they?"

"That's exactly what happened, Lily. They had no choice but to live in the desert. Every day, they had to eat the bread from heaven that God provided and drink the water from the rock. Every man—except Moses, Joshua, and Caleb—died in the desert during those long forty years. Other than Joshua and Caleb, none of those unfaithful people would ever enter the Promised Land."

"So what happened during those forty years? What was life like?" asked Anna.

"God would use this time to prepare His special nation. We always have to remember that this was all an important part of God's plan to help people find their way back to the garden and walk closely with God forever. That is really what this whole story is all about."

"So how did God prepare them?" Anna kept probing.

"Forty years of depending on God for their daily bread and water helped this group of people to learn to trust and obey God. And God used this time to reveal to Moses a great deal about His plan. Under God's direction, Moses organized the people. The men of one of the twelve tribes, the Tribe of Levi, were taught to be priests. They were taught and trained all the things about God and His Word, and it became their full-time job to be ministers to the people. Do you remember the story of Adam, when Adam began a tradition of a Grand Gathering?"

Anna replied, "That's when Adam told them all that he knew about the garden and about God and about the serpent."

"That's right, Anna. And Adam taught his son Seth that having this Grand Gathering of all the people every year was really important. Otherwise, these important stories would soon be lost. These stories were faithfully passed down from one generation to the next, and that is exactly how much of God's Word had reached Moses. But now, under God's direction, Moses had a special group of the Levites who were called the Scribes, carefully, with the help of the Holy Spirit, write down these ancient stories.

"For the first time, the Bible—God's Word—was in written form. God also had Moses begin some traditions of great festivals, where all the people would gather together on special dates. They would make animal sacrifices in repentance for their sins, and the elders would read the Bible stories. The people of the Nation of Israel were beginning to really learn about their God and how they were a special part of His plan of salvation for the world.

"After the forty long years that God kept His chosen nation in the wilderness, almost all of the adults who were a part of the Exodus had died, and most of the population had spent their entire life trusting God every day for their daily bread. This nation was now disciplined and trained in the Word of God. They trusted God, and knew that He could deliver them from any obstacle. They were now ready to enter the land that God had promised to Abraham so many years before."

Study Guide for Chapter 10 – The Exodus and the Wilderness

Story 10: The Wilderness
Read: Exodus 14–20, Numbers 13–16
Read: Papa's Story 10

After ten terrible plagues and the loss of his own son's life, Pharaoh finally lets the Israelites leave Egypt. But even then, Pharaoh decides to chase after them and bring them back.

Discussion Points and Questions

1. This part of the Bible is full of incredible miracles. Almost everybody knows the miracle of the parting of the Red Sea. Think of all the miracles involved in that.

    a. Pharaoh's army is held back by the pillar of fire.
    b. The Israelites all cross safely to the other side.
    c. Then the pillar lets Pharaoh's army chase after the Israelites.
    d. Pharaoh's entire army is drowned, and the Israelites are safe.

2. After the ten plagues and now the parting of the sea, wouldn't you think that every Israelite would be a 100 percent true believer in the God of Abraham, Isaac, and Moses?

3. Forty years is a long time. Most of the people who were alive when the Exodus from Egypt took place had died off. Now, after forty years, there is a whole nation of people who are totally dependent on God for their daily food and water. This forty-year period was not a big waste of time. During this time, God was instructing Moses to write down, for the first time, His revealed Word. This Nation

of Israel was beginning to shape up into the group of people who could fulfill some of the other promises that God had made to Abraham so long ago. What were those other promises?

Chapter 11

The Promised Land

Joshua 1–24
The Walls of Jericho
The Israelites Take Over the Land
Prophets and the Word of God

There was snow on the ground and music in the air, and it was beginning to look like Christmas. It was the Saturday before the big holiday, and Papa and Grammy were sitting in their easy chairs with a fire in the fireplace. Papa was reading a mystery novel, and Grammy was working on a crossword puzzle when the phone rang.

"It's Sally," Papa said as he read the ID on the phone. "Hi, honey. I hope everything's well at the Conroy house."

"Everything's good, Dad. But I need a break. I still have to get some gifts for the kids, and I'm running out of time. Could you and Mom watch Anna and Lily for a couple of hours while I finish up shopping? I'll bring along a Disney movie so you won't have to—"

"No, don't bring a movie," Papa interrupted. "I just finished up my next story, and I'd like the kids to hear it before Christmas. I was thinking that on Christmas Day the whole family will be together, and we could have the second Grand Gathering of the Marcus clan. I have a special story in mind for that occasion."

"That's great, Dad," said Sally, clearly relieved. "I'll drop them off with Maddie in about thirty minutes."

"That sounds great, honey. We'll see you then."

Later that morning, Lily was all set up on Papa's lap while Grammy, Anna, and the two dogs were all snuggled together on the couch. Papa began as he usually did. "Can either of you remember what the last story was about?"

"It was about the Nation of Israel living in the wilderness for forty years," Anna recalled.

"That's right, Anna. Why did God make them stay out there so long?" Papa asked.

"Because the people weren't ready to go into the Promised Land," Anna continued.

"Very good, honey. Two of the spies, Joshua and Caleb, had faith that with God's help the Israelites could take over the land. But the other ten spies didn't have faith, even after all the amazing miracles. Most of the Israelites agreed with the ten spies. The Nation of Israel still needed to learn a lot of things about their God, and this particular group of people did not have the necessary faith. It would take forty years of teaching the people about God and for them to trust God completely. A whole new generation of people would grow up in the wilderness trusting in God every day for their daily bread.

"Now after forty years, Moses had died, and Joshua was the new leader. God told Joshua that the people were finally prepared to enter into the Promised Land. Joshua moved the two million Israelites up to the banks of the Jordon River. Across the river was a large city with a strong army, the city of Jericho. In order to enter the Promised Land, the first city that the Israelites would have to defeat was Jericho.

"But the Israelites had a problem: Jericho had a large stone wall all around it. The Israelites had no effective way of fighting such a fortified city. Once again, the Nation of Israel faced an almost-impossible situation. This time, however, instead of rioting and rebelling and losing confidence, they simply looked to God for the solution to their problem. The Nation of Israel had finally learned to trust in God!

"Even though they trusted in God, they still had no idea how they were going to fight Jericho. Then God spoke to Joshua in a dream. He gave Joshua specific instructions as to how the Israelites could defeat the fortified and walled city of Jericho. When Joshua told his people God's instructions, they all agreed that it was the most unusual strategy ever for fighting a war. But they trusted God completely. So they obeyed and did exactly what He asked.

"Following God's instructions, for seven straight days, the Israelites marched completely around the city. The people of Jericho had no idea what was going on. Many of them gathered on top of the wall, and they laughed and yelled out insults to the Israelites. Then on the seventh day, after completing their march, the Israelites blew all of their trumpets. Do you know what happened?"

"I think the walls fell down, because we sing a song about Jericho in Sunday school," Lily guessed. "But I don't know much else about that story."

"I remember that song too, Lily." Papa nodded. "You're right, the walls fell down. These great big rock walls that had defended the city for hundreds of years against all kinds of powerful armies with their powerful weapons—these walls fell down because the Israelites blew their horns, just like God had requested. Not only did the walls fall down, but the entire population of Jericho was decimated. Israel completely destroyed the powerful city of Jericho without really having to fight very hard. This was clearly a miracle. The God of Israel was certainly in charge of what was going on.

"News of this incredible and totally unexpected victory spread out all over the land. God performed miracle after miracle as the Israelites captured more and more of the land. The enemies of the Israelites also learned that this God of Abraham was all-powerful. Before long, when the Canaanites saw the Israelites coming in their direction, they moved away. They didn't want to fight when they know that they would lose.

"Even though the conquest of the Promised Land was a success, the Israelites failed to obey God in two ways. First, they got tired and stopped short and failed to capture all of the land that God had promised. The people were tired of fighting, and they wanted to settle down and start enjoying their new homes. These were homes that they did not even build.

"Second, they made friends with some of the enemy and allowed them to stay in the land and live and mix with the Israelites. God knew that the false religions and evil practices of the Canaanites would be like an infection. God knew that, in time, the Israelites would accept some of these false beliefs. God had spent forty years training this special group of people to have faith in Him alone, and He didn't want that faith corrupted.

The Promises to Abraham

"Just stop and think about this, kids," Papa said. "God speaks to a man named Abraham and promises him that if he would obey God, then God would turn him into a great nation and they would live in a Promised Land. Now over five hundred years later, over two million of Abraham's descendants are living in that very land. God keeps His promises. But there was more to that promise. Can you remember what it was?"

"That the whole world would be blessed," answered Anna proudly.

"That's exactly right, Anna. Remember, kids, the Bible is God's Word to us. After Adam and Eve sinned and were kicked out of the garden, the whole story of the Bible is about God's plan to make it possible for people to return to the garden and live with Him forever. God offers a way back to the garden to every person in the world.

"My Bible is almost 1,300 pages, from Genesis to Revelation. On page 217, Joshua leads the people across the Jordan River and into the Promised Land. In the next 713 pages, my Bible tells hundreds of stories about the successes and failures of His special nation and the way they lived in the Promised Land. For over 1,450 years, God is preparing the world and the Israelites for the final part of His promise to Abraham—that is, 'the whole world would be blessed.'"

"Seven hundred thirteen pages of stories is a lot of stories," Anna observed. "What were these stories all about?"

"God still had a lot to teach the Israelites. During this time, God would choose many men to speak to. He would speak in dreams, or He would send Angels to speak to them. These men were called prophets, and many of them would write down what God told them to write. These writings were added to the writings of Moses, and during this time, the Bible was beginning to take shape."

"How did the people know that these men were really prophets and were speaking for God?" asked Anna.

"That is an excellent question. There were false prophets, and there were real prophets. God made it clear to the real ones that He was speaking to them. Their only motivation was to tell the people what God told them. Whatever they told the people always came true. If anything that they said did not come true, then they were considered to be false prophets, and they would be stoned. Oftentimes what the true prophets said was very unpopular with the people, but they said it anyway. They often told the people that they should repent and change their evil ways. Last, prophets were always very holy men, and it was clear to all the people that those men were very close to God. Unlike the real prophets, the false prophets were motivated by money, and their evilness was also clear to the people.

"Does that answer your question, Anna?"

"I think so, but what kinds of things did the prophets say?" Anna answered.

"Let me give you a couple of examples. As we have already seen over and over again, Satan is a master at deceiving the people. The Israelites were no exception, and at one point, many of the Israelites had lost their faith in God and had taken to worshiping idols the other evil practices of the native Canaanites. Several prophets would stand in the cities and call out loudly for the people to repent and return to the God of Abraham. They warned the people that if they did not repent, the barbarians would conquer them and the Israelites would be carried off into captivity."

"So what happened?" asked Lily.

"The people did not repent. They hated the prophets, and some of them were even stoned to death. But just like the prophets said, the Babylonians conquered Israel and carried the people off into captivity. Many of these prophecies would not happen until hundreds of years in the future. David, Isaiah, Malachi, Mica, and other prophets told about a coming messiah. This special person was the final part of God's great plan for the salvation of the world, and would complete God's promise to Abraham that 'the whole world would be blessed.' Altogether there were over 350 prophecies regarding this coming Savior, and this Savior is the subject of the next story.

"Right now, I think that chocolate ice cream would taste awfully good, don't you, Lily?"

Study Guide for Chapter 11 – The Promised Land

Story 11: The Promised Land
Read: Joshua 1–24
Read: Papa's Story 11

What were the things that God promised to Abraham in Genesis 12?

God had promised Abraham that if he would obey God's commands, then God would do the following:

- Make a great nation from Abraham's descendants.
- Give this nation a Promised Land.
- Bless this nation.
- Bless the whole world through this nation.

All because of Abraham's obedience.

Papa's story 11 is the story of God fulfilling the second part of the promise. Joshua will lead this "believing nation" of over two million people across the Jordan River, and they will take over the very land God had promised to Abraham so many years before.

Discussion and Questions

1. Do you remember the attitude of the Nation of Israel forty years earlier when they voted not to go into the Promised Land? Did they trust God forty years ago?
2. How is the attitude of this new Nation of Israel different? Did they trust God now? Why?
3. What do you think of the war strategy that God used to take down the powerful and walled city of Jericho? Why do you think God had such an unusual strategy? Did the people follow God's orders, even though they must have thought the orders were pretty strange?
4. How does this willingness to obey remind you of Abraham?
5. How are obedience and faith related?

6. Does it seem to you that it would be impossible for a large group of untrained, unarmed men, women, and children to take over a land of highly armed well-defended cities with trained armies? Would you call this a miracle?
7. God has now delivered on two large components of the promise that He had made to Abraham. Abraham's descendants have formed a great nation of over two million people, and they now occupy the land that Abraham had been promised.
8. God's rules of engagement in fighting a war seem pretty harsh. Joshua is told to "kill every man, woman, and child; even kill the livestock and do not take any of the precious things." Why were God's rules so harsh?
9. Do you think that this harshness could have actually saved thousands of lives in the long run?
10. What other major component of that promise still remained to be fulfilled? Do you think God keeps His promises?

Chapter 12

God's Promise to Abraham Completed

The Four Gospels: Matthew, Mark, Luke, and John
Over 350 Prophecies Fulfilled
Hundreds of Incredible Miracles
A Sinless Life, a Fantastic Teacher
Unbelievable Sacrifice, Incredible Love
The Whole World Is Blessed

Sally asked Papa if he could watch Anna for the afternoon because it was Mom's Day at Perimeter School and Sally needed to be there for Lily.

Of course Papa agreed.

"I have a bunch of questions about your story last week," Anna asked Papa once they were alone together. "You said that there were over 350 prophecies about the Savior of the world. What were some of these prophecies?"

Papa replied, "Since there are over 350 prophesies that talked about the Coming Messiah, I won't be giving you a complete answer to your question. Let me give you a short list, and then you can do your own Bible study and see how many of these you can discover on your own."

One of the most famous prophesies was written by the prophet Micah in 700 BC: "But you Bethlehem Ephrathah, though you are small among the clans of Judah, out of you will come for me one who will be ruler over Israel, whose origins are from of old, from ancient times."

Here, the Bible says that the Messiah will be from the tribe of Judah and will be born in Bethlehem.

The following are some of the most well-known:

- Isaiah 9:1–2 says that He would begin His ministry in Galilee.
- Isaiah 11:2 says that He would be despised and rejected by men, a man of sorrows, and familiar with suffering.
- Isaiah 50:6 says that He was oppressed and afflicted, and yet He did not open His mouth. He was led like a lamb to the slaughter.
- Psalm 27:12—In this verse, King David says that He would be accused by false witnesses.
- Psalm 22:16 says that His hands and feet were pierced by evil men.
- Zechariah 9:9—Here, the prophet Zechariah says that this Messiah will make a triumphal march into Jerusalem and that He will be riding on a donkey.

- Zechariah 11:12 says that He will be betrayed and sold for thirty pieces of silver.

"I could go on and on," Papa said. "But I'd rather leave it for you to research the Bible and find out for yourself. But even from this relatively short list, we can see that only Jesus of Nazareth could be the Messiah that all of these prophets are referring to. Remember all of these prophesies were made between 2,000 and 450 years before Jesus was even born. This Jesus was a Jew who lived in the Promised Land. That makes him a direct descendent of Abraham. He is the Savior that God provided for the whole world. God's promise to Abraham that the whole world will be blessed is fulfilled in Jesus Christ."

Anna looked thoughtfully at Papa and then said, "Jesus is really amazing. Tell me some more things about Him."

"You're right, Jesus was truly amazing. I can only imagine what it would have been like to see and hear Him in person. Here was a simple man, the son of a poor carpenter, who began walking the countryside talking to the people when He was about thirty years old. Before long, twelve men had dedicated their lives to following Him, crowds of thousands of people travelled great distances just to listen to Him teach, and for no clear reason, the powerful religious leaders hated Him and wanted Him dead. Remember the story of Abel and Cain? Why did Cain hate Abel so much that he wanted him dead?"

"Abel believed in God and Cain didn't?"

"That is exactly right. It's hard to understand, but until a person believes in the one true God, they don't realize it, but they are being influenced by Satan. This is Satan's kingdom. Since Adam sinned and was kicked out of the garden, everybody who is born into this world is born under the influence of Satan's evil spirit. Until they allow the Holy Spirit of the true God to enter their hearts and minds, they will, just like Satan, despise people who do believe in God. The reason Jesus came was to bring to this fallen world the kingdom of God and to make it available to all people who would believe in Him.

"To prove that He was the Son of God, Jesus performed amazing miracles. He became famous for healing people who were deathly sick. A man who was totally crippled for many years was touched by Jesus, and he was able to get up and walk.

"Over five thousand people sat on a hillside listening to Jesus teach, and when they got hungry, Jesus was able to take several fish and loaves of bread and feed the entire crowd. After they were all filled, the leftovers were gathered up, and they filled up twelve large baskets with food. Remember, God can create something simply by *thinking* it into existence. Jesus clearly demonstrated that He was God's Son. The people wanted to make Him king.

"I could go on and on about the miracles of Jesus, but I want to talk about the most important thing that He did."

"What was that, Papa?" Anna asked.

"He died on the cross. Think back on the story of Adam after he and Eve had been kicked out of the garden. One day, he called his whole family together for a Grand Gathering. Can you remember what happened at the Grand Gathering?"

"Adam told his family all about the Garden of Eden," Anna answered.

"That's right, but there was more." Papa looked at Anna.

"He also said that the evil spirit was all over this world. He also said that he misses living in the garden and that he doesn't belong here—he belongs in the garden."

"That's an excellent answer, Anna, but there was one other thing that happened at the Grand Gathering." Papa paused while Anna thought.

"I can't remember, Papa. Give me a hint."

"Remember the story that I told about you throwing the remote control and breaking your big TV?"

"How could I forget that story? It gives me the creeps every time I look at the TV." Anna laughed.

"Did we decide that your mom and dad would still love you?"

"Yes, I know that they would still love me."

"Would they forgive you?" Papa asked.

"I'm sure they would," Anna replied.

"Would there be conditions to their forgiving you?" Papa asked.

"I'd have to be sorry. Oh, I see what you're getting at now, Papa. Even though I was sorry for what I did and they forgave me, there would still be consequences for what I did. Somebody would have to pay for a new TV.

"Now I remember what happened at the end of Adam's Grand Gathering," Anna continued. "They built an altar, and the people made sacrifices for their sins."

"That's right. God wants a repentant heart. God also requires a worthy sacrifice in order for a person to be forgiven completely and get close to God again. Do you see what this has to do with the death of Jesus on a cross?" Papa asked.

"I think so," Anna answered. "Jesus's death is the sacrifice for my sins. He is my worthy sacrifice. I don't have to sacrifice a cow or a lamb."

"You get it, Anna." Papa smiled. "What else does God require of you?"

"I have to be really sorry for my sins and try to trust in Him and obey Him from now on."

"There is nothing more than I can say to you, except one thing."

"What's that, Papa?"

"I love you."

"I love you too."

The End

Note: This is the end of my story, but for Anna, it's only the beginning.

The first step in the process of salvation is for a person to understand that he/she is a sinner and in need of a savior. A savior is someone who can pay the penalty for your sins. This is called "atonement."

When Cain and Abel made their sacrifices, they were making their offerings to God to atone for their sins. Atonement is not just a sacrifice; it also requires a truly repentant heart. God knows the heart. Abel was repentant, and Cain was not. Thus, God accepted Abel's offering but not Cain's.

Jesus is the Lamb of God. He is the sacrifice for our sins (all those who trust in Him). Like Anna, we need to come before God with a repentant heart and accept the sacrifice that He made on our behalf. This is what Anna has done.

Now the great adventure of living a life for Christ begins. For sure, Anna is forgiven, but she's still a sinner. For the rest of her life she will go through a process of becoming more and more like Christ in her thinking and actions. This is called "sanctification." Anna's natural spirit and the Holy Spirit will oftentimes clash and disagree, but the more Anna submits her will over to God's will, the more she will grow into the eternal person God wants her to be.

Study Guide for Chapter 12 – The Promise Completed

Story 12: The Promise Completed
Read: Papa's Story 12
Read: God's Promise to Abraham (Gen. 12:1–3)

Papa's story 12 is the story of God fulfilling the third and fourth parts of the promise. This special nation, now living in their own Promised Land, was living in a very evil and hostile world where Satan had deceived almost all the people. Only Israel, of all the nations on earth, had been given special insight into who the One True God was. They now had the written Word of God. Over time, this Word would grow as Israel continued to produce special men of God who were called prophets. Papa's story 12 is the story of how God fulfills his promise to Abraham.

Discussion and Questions

This chapter concludes *Papa's Stories*, and as far as I (Papa) am concerned, it says it all. Read this chapter over with your child, and have a great discussion. Hopefully, these stories have given you some special opportunities to spend quality time together and talk about these very important things. This could be the most significant and important time that you could ever spend together.

PAPA'S STORIES

Papa Answers His Granddaughters' Questions

Lily's Question: If God already knows everything and He never changes, what good does it do me to pray? I can't change God's mind, can I?

Papa's Answer: There are three really good reasons to pray.

1. *Prayer is communication,* and communication builds relationships. The more you talk with God, the closer you'll become to Him. The closer you become, the better you will understand what He wants of you, and what you desire will begin to line up with His will.
2. *Prayer brings peace* in your heart. When we cry out to God about something that's bothering us, we start to trust Him with the solutions, and we are comforted, knowing that He loves us and that He will work out everything for our benefit.
3. *Prayer brings results.* We are changed by our prayers. God changes us—He isn't the one who is changed. However, anyone who prays regularly will know that many times God honors their prayers with the desired results. God does answer prayer. Sometimes His answer is no, but by praying, we can know that no is the answer that is best for us.

Anna's Question: Papa, I've been thinking about something. Many of the stories that you've told us begin with God talking to somebody, telling them to do something. God spoke to Adam and Eve in the garden, then later God told Adam to hold the Great Gathering and tell his family about the garden. Then God spoke to Noah and told him to build the ark. God spoke to Abraham and told him to leave his country, and then God promised Abraham that he would be the father of a great nation and be a blessing to the world. God spoke to Moses, and Daniel, and Joseph, and Mary, and Paul. I've never heard God talk to me. How does God talk to people?

Papa's Answer: God speaks to people in many different ways.

1. *Our hearts.* The Bible says that we are born with a knowledge of God written in our hearts. We all have a sense of right and wrong. When you're about to disobey what your mother has told you and you get nervous and feel bad, that's God talking to you.
2. *Prophets and the Word.* Ever since Adam, God has spoken to people by choosing certain men and women to know things about God, and He wants them to tell the people these things. These special men and women are called prophets. The Word of God—we call it the Bible—was written by these prophets, and it can be trusted. Everything in it is true. If the Bible clearly says something, then you can consider that those words are the words of God and He is talking straight to you. For instance, if it says, "Children, obey your parents," then you could rightly say, "God told me to obey my parents."
3. *Dreams.* God has spoken to people through dreams. Two examples of God speaking through dreams are of Daniel, before he faced the lions, and of Joseph, the son of Jacob. Many other prophets had dreams, and they clearly understood these dreams to be God speaking to them.
4. *Angels.* There are many Bible stories that tell of an angel appearing to a person. Mary, Joseph, and Paul were all visited by angels.

Anna's Question: I have a friend in the neighborhood who is a Muslim. She says that she is saved because she believes in Mohammed. But she also says that I can be saved because I believe in Jesus. She says that it really doesn't matter who you believe in, just that you believe in somebody.

Papa's Answer: Many people like to think that way; it's a very popular and politically correct thing to say in today's society. It doesn't offend anyone, even someone who believes sincerely in the

Sun God, or the God of the Trees, or that Mother Nature is God. If I believe sincerely that I am God, then by her definition, I am saved.

Consider the following verses. These are the words of Jesus:

- For God so loved the world that He gave His one and only Son, that whoever believes in him shall not perish but have eternal life.
- I am the way, the truth, and the life. No man comes to the Father but by me.

In these verses, Jesus clearly eliminates all other religious leaders as potential "saviors."

Then consider the following facts:

- For several thousand years, prophets made over 350 predictions about the coming Messiah. Many of these predictions were very precise. For instance, in the year 700 BC, long before Jesus was even born, the prophet Micah said that this Savior would be born in the town of Bethlehem and that He would be of the Tribe of Judah. Jesus fulfilled all of the prophecies, and no other person on the planet (including Muhammad) came even close.
- The record of Jesus's life was amazing. He healed blind people, He healed people with leprosy, He raised Lazarus from the dead, He fed over five thousand people with only several fish and loaves of bread, He walked on water and calmed the storm, and on and on. After He was crucified, He rose again from the dead. He was the Son of God, and He proved it with every aspect of His life.

Anna's Response: I believe that Jesus is the Only Way, but what do I say to my friend? She really thinks that Mohammed is the Savior.

Papa's Answer: That is a great question. I'm not sure what the perfect answer is, but I have learned several things about witnessing over the years. Much of what I've learned is what *not* to do.

- *Pray.* Pray for her. In the end, only God can change her heart to see the truth.
- *Love.* Love her. Be a great friend. Let her see the love of Jesus living in you.
- *Don't argue.* Don't argue with her over Jesus versus Mohammed and which one is the real savior. I've learned many times that you can't win arguments like that. You only harden their hearts and make further conversation more difficult.
- *Witness.* In as nice and nonthreatening way as possible, you can let her know that you do believe that Jesus is the Savior. If the opportunity presents itself, you can point out some of the reasons why you believe that: the fulfilled prophecies, the miracles, His sacrifice on the cross for our sins, and His resurrection. If God has opened her heart and mind, she may realize that Mohammed didn't die for her sins, and he wasn't famous for doing any miracles, and he never rose from the dead. But Jesus did. She too can be saved.

PAPA'S STORIES

How Papa Sees It

I feel that I owe the reader more detail and comment about some of the ideas that I have expressed during these stories.

These stories are written with one primary purpose: I want to leave my own children and grandchildren the most important legacy that I can. If in telling these stories I can help them to understand and believe God's Word, then my purpose is fulfilled.

Clearly I have taken some liberties with my interpretation of the Bible. For instance, the idea of Adam's Grand Gathering was mine. The Bible (Genesis 3) does teach that Adam and Eve walked and talked with God every day in the garden. Thus, Adam knew God with a guilt-free and sinless mind. He could really *know* God. Every other person on this planet, since Adam, knows God through the cloud of sin that clutters each of our lives.

Genesis 5 teaches us that Seth, Adam's third son, was the second Patriarch, and that the Word was passed down from generation to generation all the way down from Adam to Noah, from Noah to Abraham, and then Isaac, and, finally, Jacob. At that point, some twenty-two generations after Adam, the Nation of Israel was formed, and God would continue passing His Word down through a series of prophets.

Adam's first two sons were Cain and Abel. Genesis 4 clearly shows that of Adam's first two sons, only 50 percent were believers. The fact that God accepted Abel's sin offering indicates that Abel had a repentant heart and desired to obey God. Abel believed in God. That God rejected Cain's offering indicates that Cain did not have a repentant heart nor did he desire to know God. We have to assume that Adam taught each of his first two sons about God and Creation. Only one believed, the other did not.

As I read Genesis 5, I get a clear sense that each Patriarch diligently carried God's Word down to the next Patriarch in the generational line. Genesis 5 also says that each Patriarch had many other sons and daughters, in addition to the chosen one. The Bible also says that by the time we get to Noah, only one man could be found in all the population of the earth who had a heart for God.

It is very clear that in those days a great majority of the people on earth were rejecting the Word of God. Satan's Spirit was clearly winning the hearts of most of the people. But God did preserve a small remnant. When I look at the state of our world today, I think it is fair to say that Satan's influence is as widespread and powerful as it ever was.

Creation and Evolution

When I was in high school, I can clearly remember something from my biology class. There was a twenty-foot-long chart on top of the blackboard, titled "The Evolution of Man." This chart began on the left with some monkeylike creature on all fours, the next prehuman animal had somehow stood up on his two feet, but in every other way, this naked beast looked just like a monkey. As we looked from left to right across this chart, each creature in line looked more and more like the man at the far right. He was standing, proudly carrying a briefcase and wearing a Brooks Brother suit. With a nifty series of mutations, the animal kingdom kept improving until finally modern man had arrived. I had always thought that mutations were "bad" things. I can't imagine a mother holding up her newborn baby and happily proclaiming, "Look here at my beautiful little mutant." But apparently I was wrong.

As the biology course progressed, we read about the "scientific study" in England where black moths and white moths were carefully observed by experts. These scientists observed that this population of moths all turned black—the birds were eating the white ones because they couldn't hide on the soot-blackened trees. Then after the trains stopped pouring out the black soot, the trees lightened up again, and once again, the white moths returned to their previous percentage of the moth population. After some explanation, the conclusion of these experts was this was proof of the theory of evolution.

Of course, whether or not they were black or white, all the time, we were talking about moths. I never could understand how that study could somehow prove evolution. There were other interesting "proofs" in our textbook: one proof had to do with the giraffe's long neck evolving because the only food available was the leaves at the top of trees.

I was sixteen years old and a pretty good student. I assumed that the teachers and the textbooks were sources of accurate knowledge, and so I accepted the theory of evolution as a simple fact of life.

My experiences in chemistry, biology, philosophy, and other courses at the University of Michigan all served to support this theory of evolution. As a matter of fact, by the late 1960s, evolution was being taught as a fact, not as a theory. Anybody who challenged this "fact" was severely criticized and ridiculed as some kind of religious nutcase. I was certainly not one who wanted to be thought of that way. As my worldview took shape, I was pretty convinced the biblical story of Creation was nothing but a myth and that the Bible—and Christianity—was just a bunch of good ideas for people who liked that kind of thing.

I graduated from the U of M, became a tennis pro, began managing tennis clubs, and in 1970, I married my high school sweetheart, Donna. Donna and I had two beautiful girls, and in 1979, we were living in Fort Lauderdale, Florida, where I ran a large tennis complex.

I had no interest in God, but I did have an instinct that there was something missing in my life, and I was starting to question what my purpose for living was. At just the right time, Donna and I were invited to attend a church, and for some reason, we accepted the invite. Something amazing happened to both of us. As we sat in the large auditorium, we both clearly heard the message from the pulpit. Our hearts were both broken and healed. Broken from the guilt of our own sin, and healed by the saving grace of Jesus Christ. There was no doubt in my mind that I had found the truth and that I was now a child of God. Donna had the same exact response to God's Word.

I became an avid reader overnight. Within eight weeks, I had read the entire Bible, sometimes staying up all night. I was totally fascinated, and couldn't get enough of it. But I still had a lot to learn.

I was becoming ever more aware that there was a spiritual war going on—right here on planet Earth, even in my own heart. Satan is alive and well, and never stops trying to deceive us.

Then something happened that really shook me up, and was my greatest challenge. Dr. James Kennedy was the pastor of my church, and there was no person on this planet I trusted more. One Sunday, he taught a sermon that totally blasted the theory of evolution. He said that evolution was one of the greatest deceptions that Satan had ever used to prevent man from finding the truth. Evolution was a lie, and he challenged every aspect of it. Basically, he explained that evolution is totally incompatible with the clear teachings of the Bible. If evolution is true, then the Bible is false.

I was challenged. Even when I had recently read the Bible, my reading of Genesis was pretty shallow, and in my own mind, I considered it to be a nice fairy tale—nothing but a nice and colorful introduction to the Bible. In my mind, the Bible actually began in Genesis 4.

Now you have to know something about me. I always excelled in mathematics. I especially loved "proofs," the logical deduction of step-by-step proof. I took several courses in graduate school in Logical Deduction and Argument Theory. Another course, the Theory of Mathematics, dealt with proving all kinds of things. Now, I had a chance to use all of these theories to prove to myself the truth of Christianity or the truth of evolution.

I went to bookstores and libraries. Soon, I had accumulated a large library, including all kinds of books on evolution as well as a number of books blasting the theory of evolution. What surprised me the most was when I visited a Christian bookstore and found a whole section of books on Creation versus evolution. Clearly, I was not the only person challenged by this problem.

This time, as I studied evolution, I would not just accept what the author stated as "scientific fact" just because he said it was. I determined that I would look at the so-called evidence and judge for myself if it was, in fact, evidence of macroevolution.

Also, as I read, I learned that the word *evolution* can mean different things. *Microevolution* is variation within a species, and is happening all the time. There are countless examples of microevolution, and virtually everybody accepts microevolution as proven fact.

Macroevolution is something altogether different. The theory of macroevolution declares that over time and throughout history species have evolved into different species. Macroevolution claims that every species that we see today, including man, evolved from some "lower" life form. The believers in this theory claim that there are countless examples of macroevolution. However, when pressed, they always point to well-known examples of microevolution. They claim that given enough time, this same process will lead to new species.

They make this claim with no supporting evidence. There are no real examples of macroevolution. Rather than arguing the creation-versus-evolution debate here, I will conclude by saying that I am totally convinced that God created all things, just like the Bible teaches, and that macroevolution is not at all true and there is no supporting evidence of it ever having happened.

My daughter Katie recently had her second daughter. As I held this precious tiny baby, I looked closely at those perfect little fingers and toes, the delicate nose and ears, those beautiful eyes, and I thought of all the other incredible wonders that this little person embodied. I stand humbly in awe of the incredible Creator. It's hard for me to think that this remarkable little person could be nothing but the result of chemical chance and lots of time and thousands of mutations. That "evolutionary position" is not demonstrated or backed by any evidence. That belief requires a willingness to disrespect the real Creator of the Universe. The True Creator must be astounded at the arrogance of sinful man. I know for sure that Satan revels in his successful deception.

Please recall Papa's story 5, the story of Cain and Abel. In that story, Cain thought that his father, Adam, had lost his mind. Cain saw the Creation Story as utter nonsense. I am sure that many of my nonbelieving friends view me and my belief in Creation as being crazy. I can only pray that one day, their eyes will be opened and they will have ears to hear the truth. I humbly ask of them, if you believe in evolution, follow the rules of science and logic and show me the proof. Just show me one example of macroevolution, and you can win the argument. Until you do that, please don't think of me as a nimcomepoop.

What amazes me is that very few, if any, of these nonbelievers will take up my challenge. It is clear that another tactic that Satan uses is to affect nonbelievers with a spirit of apathy. They just don't care. It doesn't seem important to them. They could care less if some God created Adam from the dust of the ground, or if their great-great-great-grandfather was a monkey.

To My Nonbeliever Friends

I've been asked, "Now that you're a saved Christian and I'm not, do you feel that you're a better person than me?"

My answer is, "Absolutely not! The fact of my salvation was not in any way based on some goodness in me. I simply believed God's Word. I believe that God sent His Son to walk among us and teach the truth. He demonstrated exactly who He was many times with incredible miracles. I believe that He died a horrible death on the cross as a sin offering for all my sins, and with a repentant heart, I accept this free gift. Once again, he demonstrated exactly who He was when He rose from the dead, just like He said He would. I believe that I will spend eternity with God, not because of my goodness but because I believe in Jesus and what He taught and what He did for me."

Today, some thirty-plus years since I became a Christian, I still struggle with anger, greed, hate, forgiving people who wrong me, foul language, impatience, lust—need I go on? But I do believe that I'm not nearly as "bad" as I was before I was saved. Slowly, I have developed a better ability to submit to God's will and not to give in to the temptations of the evil one. But I'm still a sinner, and I'm sure I'll be a sinner until the day I die. But on the Judgment Day, God will not see my sins; He will see the perfect righteousness of Jesus Christ.

God's Plan of Salvation

Throughout these stories, I have referred to God's plan of salvation. Here I give a short summary of what I mean by that.

1. God created all things, and His crown of Creation (primary purpose) was man. It was God's intent to create a large group of people who would *willfully choose* to love and obey Him forever. Man had to have free will in order to willfully choose. Even before the beginning of time, God knew that all men would fall to Satan's temptations and choose to disobey. But God had a plan so that any man could willfully choose to join with God in a perfect and eternal relationship. The Old Testament is the story of God executing that plan.
2. In Genesis 3, after Adam and Eve disobeyed, God spoke directly to Satan, and He said, "I will put enmity between you and the woman, and between your offspring and hers, he will crush your head and you will strike his heal." Here God tells Adam, Eve, and Satan the end game. One day, the offspring of the woman will clash with Satan. The result will be that Satan will cause pain and suffering, but the woman's offspring (Jesus) will ultimately prevail by crushing Satan's head.
3. Genesis 4 through 9 shows the total depravity of man. God did reserve for himself a small remnant of people who would have a desire to know, love, and obey God. Noah was such a man.
4. Then in Genesis 12, God makes a promise to a man called Abram. If Abram would obey God, God would do the following:

    a. Make Abram's offspring into a great nation of people,
    b. Abram would be blessed and be a blessing, and his name would be great.

c. This nation would have a beautiful Promised Land to occupy.
   d. And finally, all the nations on the earth would be blessed through him.

5. The remainder of the Old Testament is the long story of God's keeping His promise to Abram. Despite incredible odds, Abram's family grew into a great nation. With many miraculous signs, this nation of Israel occupied a beautiful Promised Land. Ultimately, after hundreds of prophesies, a virgin woman conceived the promised Savior of the world. Jesus was this Savior, and his life, death, and resurrection are the fulfillment of God's promise.
6. God's salvation is a free gift to all who will willfully choose.

About the Author

Brian grew up in Holland, Michigan. He graduated with a degree in economics from the University of Michigan and has been married to his high school sweetheart, Donna, for forty-seven years.

By ten years old, Brian was the Holland City tennis champ, and at thirteen, he won the Michigan State junior tournament, qualifying for the nationals. At seventeen, he won the National 18's Indoor Doubles title, and shortly thereafter, he signed a full scholarship to play tennis at the U of M.

In 1980, Brian and Donna were invited to a church where they both heard and responded to the Gospel for the first time. Ever since then, they have been growing in their faith, and for the past twenty-six years, Brian has served as an elder in Perimeter Church in Duluth, Georgia.

Brian and Donna have three married daughters and seven beautiful grand-daughters.

CPSIA information can be obtained
at www.ICGtesting.com
Printed in the USA
LVOW05s1736090916
503821LV00025B/181/P